Philip Johannes Nel

The Structure and Ethos
of the Wisdom Admonitions in Proverbs

Philip Johannes Nel

The Structure and Ethos of the Wisdom Admonitions in Proverbs

Walter de Gruyter · Berlin · New York
1982

Beiheft zur Zeitschrift für die alttestamentliche Wissenschaft

Herausgegeben von Georg Fohrer

158

CIP-Kurztitelaufnahme der Deutschen Bibliothek

Nel, Philip Johannes:
The structure and ethos of the wisdom admonitions in proverbs /
Philip Johannes Nel. – Berlin ; New York : de Gruyter, 1982.
    (Beiheft zur Zeitschrift für die alttestamentliche Wissenschaft ;
    158)
    ISBN 3-11-008750-2
NE: Zeitschrift für die alttestamentliche Wissenschaft / Beiheft

©

1982

Preface

It is with great pleasure that I make mention of the following people by reason of their contribution towards the completion of this study.

First of all, my profound appreciation and gratitude to my promotor, Prof F. C. Fensham for his contribution, one I consider 'parental' to my academic forming. I am grateful for his sustained interest, encouragement, guidance and counsel without which this study could not have been completed.

Secondly, I wish to thank Prof H. Gese, (University of Tübingen, West Germany), for his indispensible contribution as external examiner. His stimulating ideas and good counsel will not escape the attentive readers.

I am sincerely grateful to Dr W. T. Claassen for his part as examiner.

Then too, I wish to express my appreciation to Prof F. du T. Laubscher, head of the department of Semitic Languages at the UOFS, both for his interest and his kind consideration during the completion of this study.

I am grateful to Drs P. Brouwer for his revision of this study's text with a view to English idiom.

I also with to thank the Council of the University of the Orange Free State for the special study leave granted to me and for their financial assistance in the completion of this study.

I also gratefully acknowledge receipt of financial assistance from the Human Sciences Research Council, which helps to make this publication possible.

Finally, my gratitude and appreciation for the self-effacing assistance offered by my wife and children. Therefore it gives me great pleasure to dedicate this study to my wife.

Above all, I give thanks to God who makes each day of work a day of joy.

Contents

Abbreviations

AION	Annali del'Instituto Orientale di Napoli.
ANET	Ancient Near Eastern Texts relating to the Old Testament.
August	Augustinianum
Bibl	Biblica
Bib Or	Bibliotheca Orientalis
BS	Biblische Studien
Bible Trans	The Bible Translator.
BWL	Babylonian Wisdom Literature
BWANT	Beiträge zur Wissenschaft vom Alten und Neuen Testament
BZAW	Beihefte zur Zeitschrift für die alttestamentliche Wissenschaft
BZ	Biblische Zeitschrift
CBQ	Catholic Biblical Quarterly
Ev Quart	The Evangelical Quarterly
EV Th	Evangelische Theologie
FS	Festschrift
HUCA	Hebrew Union College Annual
IrTQ	Irish Theological Quarterly
IEJ	Israel Exploration Journal
JAOS	Journal of the American Oriental Society
JBL	Journal of Biblical Literature
JBR	Journal of Bible and Religion
JCS	Journal of Cuneiform Studies
JNES	Journal of Near Eastern Studies
JNSL	Journal of Northwest Semitic Languages
JQR	Jewish Quarterly Review
JTS	Journal of Theological Studies
KS	Kleine Schrifte zur Geschichte des Volkes Israel
NGTT	Nederduits-Gereformeerde Teologiese Tydskrif
NThT	Nederlands Theologisch Tijdschrift
NZSThR	Neue Zeitschrift für Systematische Theologie und Religionsphilosophie
OA	Oriens Antiquus
OTLib	Old Testament Library
OTS	Oud Testamentische Studien
OTWSA	Ou Testamentiese Werkgemeenskap van Suid-Afrika
RGG	Die Religion in Geschichte und Gegenwart
SAV	Schweizerisches Archiv für Volkskunde
SBT	Studies in Biblical Theology
SJT	Scottish Journal of Theology
ThLZ	Theologische Literaturzeitung
ThRNF	Theologische Rundschau Neue Folge
ThWNT	Theologisches Wörterbuch zum Neuen Testament
VT	Vetus Testamentum

VTS	Supplements to Vetus Testamentum
WMANT	Wissenschaftliche Monographien zum Alten und Neuen Testament
WO	Welt des Orients
ZAW	Zeitschrift für alttestamentliche Wissenschaft
ZThK	Zeitschrift für Theologie und Kirche

Transliteration*

Consonants

א = ʾ	ה = h	כ = k	צ = ṣ
ב = b	ו = w	ל = l	ק = q
ב = b	ז = z	מ = m	ר = r
ג = g	ח = ḥ	נ = n	שׂ = ś
ג = g	ט = ṭ	ס = s	שׁ = š
ד = d	י = y	פ = p	ת = t
ד = d	כ = k	פ = p	ת = t

Vowels

ַ = a	ֹ = ō	ֳ = ă	ָ = ā
ֵ = ɛ	ֻ = u	ָ = ŏ	ֵ = ē
ִ = i	ְ = ě	ֱ = ɛ̆	וּ = û

ָ + matres lectionis = â
ֶ + matres lectionis = ê
ִ + matres lectionis = î
ֵ + matres lectionis = ê
ֹ + matres lectionis = ô

---

* Conjugated forms of verbs with a final weak consonant are transliterated with the last radical.

Chapter 1: Introduction

1.1 The Wisdom Literature of Israel

»Wisdom« (whatever the controversies attending the concept) desig-
nates a collective literary phenomenon of the Ancient Near East. The most
peculiar feature of that wisdom is its educational or pedagogic quality,
which is not nearly so pronouncedly the character of the priestly and
prophetic literature.

The explication of wisdom in the form of proverbs is one of the most
elementary literary expressions of man's insight into his environment and
experience of the world (world-and-life-view). This appears most plainly in
primitive cultures in which individual existence is part and parcel of the
cosmic order. The skilfull gathering of this knowledge (wisdom) in the
form of proverbs or ethical prescriptions, reflects the importance of this
wisdom for the individual who is constantly aiming at an »orderly« understanding of his existence within the comprehensive cosmic order. It is
therefore quite logical that the earliest literary manifestation of this wisdom
(Egypt and Mesopotamia) would reflect a pedagogical character. Eventually
this wisdom played a major part in institutional education.

Knowledge of reality and experience of the world correlate to a great
extent with the nature of Ancient Near Eastern cultures. It is therefore
justifiable to maintain that this wisdom, which reflects world experience, is
a collective phenomenon of the Ancient Near East. This assumption obviously does not exclude the features peculiar to each culture. At the same
time each culture can display characteristics common to all without
jeopardizing. Accordingly, wisdom may well have its own tradition in
Israel including a theological development peculiar to itself. It is therefore
very naive to maintain that wisdom is a non-Israelite tradition which is
totaly irreconcilable with Jahwism[1].

There is no reason to question the authenticity of the traditional view
which relates the wisdom tradition to the period of Solomon[2]. We might,
however, assume that wisdom proverbs (especially popular proverbs)
existed before Solomon, but one can hardly conceive of a fixed wisdom
tradition before the monarchy with its official administration. The

---

[1] Cf. Preuss, H. D., EvTh 30 (1970), 393—417.
[2] Cf. Mettinger, T. N. D., Solomonic State Officials, 1971, 140ff.; Harrington, W., IrTQ 34
(1963), 313ff., and Skladny, U., Die ältesten Spruchsammlungen in Israel, 1962, 84ff.

monarchy created new official institutions and professional positions such
as the scribe. The art of writing came into use not only for administrative
purposes (annals), but also for scientific activity, such as onomastica (cf. 1
Kings 5:13). Also the »humanities« found their first literary cristallization
of expression. Solomon's contribution to the corpus of wisdom literature is
therefore beyond doubt. The extent of Egyptian influence[3] is as yet too difficult to establish with certainty.

The collection of proverbs in the familiar literary form seems to have
flourished during the reign of Hezekiah[4]. According to W. F. Albright this
literary renaissance was stimulated by Phoenician influence[5].

The established wisdom tradition underwent crucial theological
renewal during the Persian period (cf. Prov 1−9 and Job) and the Greek
period (cf. Sirach and Qoheleth (?)). This renewal continued until New
Testament times[6]. Thus, the wisdom tradition became established in Israel
as a tradition in its own right amongst the traditions of Law, Covenant,
Prophets, etc. For centuries the development of the wisdom tradition was
the Cinderella of Old Testament research, and even today it is not fully
documented.

The following literary works of Biblical tradition are generally
accepted as wisdom literature: Proverbs, Job, Ecclesiastes, Sirach and
Sapientia Solomonis. Quite a number of Psalms are classified as »wisdom
Psalms«[7] and the works of Tobit and Baruch, although not direct
educational literature, reflect wisdom influence.

Mowinckel's use of the term »wisdom Psalms« has come in for
criticism[8]. It is true that most of the so-called »wisdom Psalms« can be
classified within the frame of the known Psalm-genres. Although in a few
cases, several Psalms do treat typical wisdom topics in a clearly didactic
manner (eg. Ps 37 and 49); hence the term »wisdom Psalms« is justifiable.

---

[3] Cf. eg. the latest discussion on Prov 22 17−24 22 and the Egyptian Amenemope in Grumach, I, Untersuchungen zur Lebenslehre des Amenemope, 1972.

[4] Cf. Collection E of Prov. Cf. also the recognition of Hezekiah's position in the Baba
Bathra 14−15 (Babylonian Talmud).

[5] Albright, W. F., VTS 3, 1965, 1−15. The Canaanite influence on Biblical wisdom is attested by various scholars: cf. Dahood, M., Bibl 33 (1952), 30−52; Proverbs and the
Northwest Semitic Philology, 1963, and Northwest Semitic Philology and Job, in: The
Bible in Current Catholic Thought, 1962, 55−74; Feinberg, Ch. L., Ugaritic Literature
and the Book of Job (Diss.), 1945, and Story, C. I. K., JBL 64 (1945), 319−337.

[6] Cf. Gese, H., Vom Sinai zum Zion, 1974, 168−179, and Beiträge zur Biblischen
Theologie, 1977, 152−201.

[7] Psalms classified with a certain wisdom influence are: Pss 1.9.10.12.14.15.17.36.37.49.
52.73.91.94.112.119.127.128 and 139.

[8] Mowinckel, S., VTS 3, 1955, 205−224.

A large number of articles were published lately to testify wisdom influence in other parts of Biblical literature[9].

According to B. Childs[10] Is 14 22–27 17 14b and 28 29 are specimens of what he calls »Summary-appraisal« – a genre he attributes to the wisdom literature. The presumedly didactic character of these sayings causes Childs to classify them as part of the wisdom tradition. Childs, however, did not demonstrate beyond doubt that this form is peculiar to the wisdom tradition.

It seems necessary to warn against an exaggeration of the wisdom influence in Biblical literature and a concomitant tendency to note wisdom influence and wisdom forms indiscriminately at the least suggestion. Wisdom influence may not be assumed wherever we find self-reflection (anthropological and psychological) in literature. According to such a wide description the greater part of the Old Testament can be classified as wisdom literature. The Book of Daniel is not as such to be classified as wisdom literature or under wisdom influence simply because of the fact that an innocent man's suffering (traditional topic of the wisdom literature) occurs in Daniel? Traditional wisdom literature also reflects influences of the prophetic, Deuteronomistic and priestly traditions. But that does not mean that these »influenced pieces« are Deuteronomistic history, prophetic sayings or priestly stipulations. This mutual influence of traditions upon each other must be recognized without leading us to forced literary classifications.

1.2 Discussion of Problems and Aims

As is evident from the title, this thesis concerns itself with two aspects of the wisdom admonitions in the Book of Proverbs, viz. the structure and interpretation (ethos) of the wisdom admonitions. Both concerns, however, have been variously treated in a large number of discussions, but no views expressed have been adequate for the settling of the controversies and differences in this regard. Though this thesis does not pretend to provide all the answers, it does attempt to clarify certain issues and methodological matters in this area and help to clear the way towards a tenable view.

---

[9] Cf. Crenshaw, J. L., JBL 88 (1969), 129–142, and Studies in Ancient Israelite Wisdom, 1976, 9ff.; Alonso-Schökel, L., Bibl 43 (1962), 295–316; McKenzie, J. L., JBL 86 (1967), 1–9; Schmidt, W. H., WMANT 17, 1967, 32–48; Weinfeld, M., JBL 86 (1967), 249ff.; Wolff, H. W., Amos' geistige Heimat, 1964; Von Rad, G., VTS 1, 1953, 120–127; Hermission, H.-J., Probleme Biblischer Theologie (FS. G. von Rad), 1971, 137–154, and Boston, J., JBL 87 (1968), 198–202.

[10] Childs, B. S., Isaiah and the Assyrian Crisis, 1967, 129–136.

With regard to the formal structure of the wisdom admonition there exists no extensive description of this genre as found in Proverbs. There is no consensus that there is such a genre of wisdom admonition. Studies published to date classify certain structural devices found in Proverbs with various genres proper to other traditions[11].

We must, therefore, first provide a description of the admonition and compare it with the *tôrâ*-stipulation.

Past description of the admonition was entirely based on the linguistic formulation of the admonition, with very little reference to the connected motivative clause. As will be demonstrated at a later stage this customary approach is totally unacceptable. Hence, a discussion of the role and function of the motivative clause in the admonition is essential for a proper understanding of both the formal structure of the admonition and its interpretation.

Several answers have been given in the past on the life-setting (Sitz im Leben) of the wisdom admonitions (cf. later). These views must be evaluated in terms of the grounds provided for them. We must also enquire whether the authoritative character of the wisdom admonitions is directly related to their setting in life (as accepted by the majority of scholars) or consists in something else.

Major problems arise when dealing with the interpretation of the wisdom admonitions and of the wisdom sayings as a whole. One must be careful not to interpret the wisdom literature of Israel solely on the basis of »wisdom« as an international phenomenon. Similarities and identical formulations there are, but without clearly detracting from the peculiar character of each culture. Identity in formulation is not necessarily an identity of content. Similar features in different cultures are for their interpretation to be seen in relation to the peculiarities of each culture.

A considerable body of literature exists on the interpretation of the wisdom literature, including the admonitions. It is my impression that by and large too much has been made of the distinction between the theological context of the wisdom literature and that of other Biblical literature[12].

The views expressed, moreover, have been dominated by the so-called »Gattungsgeschichte« as is apparent from the studies of Gerstenberger and Richter already referred to. I by no means deny the function and value of the »gattungsgeschichtliche« method in the field of literary criticism, nor its function in determining a genre's life-setting, but, for interpretation, the life-setting of a genre in Biblical literature is not a sound enough criterion.

---

[11] Cf. the Treatment of the so-called »Vetitiv« and »Prohibitiv« by Richter, W., Recht und Ethos: Versuch einer Ortung des weisheitlichen Mahnspruches, 1966, and Gerstenberger, E., Wesen und Herkunft des apodiktischen Rechts, 1965.

[12] Cf. Zimmerli, W., Les Sagesses du Proche−Orient Ancient, 1962, 121 and 127−130.

Other features must be taken into consideration with regard to the wisdom admonitions as well: For example, the semantic references in the motivative clauses of the admonitions; then too, the development of the wisdom tradition in the various literary collections and last, but not least, we must take account of the dominant religious principle. This religious principle must not be characterised from a systematic theological point of view only, but its nature must be established from the formal contents and functioning of this genre within the religious community of Israel.

These aspects will be emphasized in an interpretation of the ethos of the wisdom admonitions against the backdrop of the results achieved from our linguistic analyses.

It may be objected that I neglect the non-biblical wisdom literature. But for our purpose, there is no reason to discuss all non-biblical wisdom literature at length. It will not be ignored altogether, but extensive treatment is beyond the premises of this study. These introductory comments, clearly, admit that no adequate understanding of the Biblical wisdom literature is possible without a thorough knowledge of the non-biblical wisdom literature.

Requisites of scope require that this study be limited to the form and number of the admonitions in the Book of Proverbs. That again does not mean that the admonitions in other biblical wisdom literature are ignored. They are, however, not expressly dealt with. It is assumed that the classification of the admonitions in Proverbs is broad enough to accommodate the admonitions in the other biblical wisdom literature. Notable differences in form and development will be referred to.

1.3 Method of Study

As formulated in the title of this thesis we intend an extensive analysis, categorisation and description of the wisdom admonitions in the book Proverbs. The categorisation will be done in the light of the connected motivative clauses for two main reasons:

a) Because of the absolute importance of the motivative clause for the admonition (as would become clear from the previous paragraph). These clauses may no longer be ignored in any description of the admonition and they are of vital importance to the interpretation. Previous descriptions have by and large neglected this aspect.

b) Because I recognise the distinctive formulations within the admonition itself to be structural devices of one inclusive genre, not instances of different genres (Gattungen). To be more precise: The so-called »Prohibitiv« and »Vetitiv« forms (cf. the studies of Gerstenberger and Richter which we referred to earlier) are not genres (Gattungen), but only structural variation within the genre of the wisdom admonition.

We will, however, pay due attention to these different devices employed in the various admonitions and determine the frequency with which the various forms occur and whether a form-historical (formgeschichtliche) development can be obtained.

The description and categorization of the admonitions will take their context, as provided by the nine major collections in Proverbs, into account[13]:

A Prov 1—9
B Prov 10—22 16
C Prov 22 17—24 22
D Prov 24 23—34
E Prov 25—29
F Prov 30 1—15
G Prov 30 15ff.
H Prov 31 1—9
I   Prov 31 10—31[14]

The life-setting of the wisdom admonitions will be determined not only by linguistic analysis, but also by the ethos expressed in the various admonitions *and* wisdom-sayings (Aussage). An absolute distinction in this respect is impossible (as will be seen in the paragraph concerning the relations between admonition and »Aussage«).

With regard to the interpretation of the admonition and its ethos the field broadens and the total context of the sentence-literature will have to be considered.

The last chapter of this study advances only preliminary suggestions in support of a hypothesis concerning the initiative or forceful imperative behind the wisdom-ethos. What is the motivating requirement of the ethos? It leads us into a discussion of theological matters of great importance concerning evil, sin, anthropology, natural theology, etc. Wisdom research to date has not taken adequate account of these issues, in fact it has ignored them. We hope that these suggestions, based on a considerable number of sayings in the wisdom literature, will stimulate further research in this field.

---

[13] This too is done to account for form-historical development and is important with a view to interpretation.

[14] Cf. Fohrer, G., Einleitung in das A. T., 1965, 348 ff.; Kaiser, O., Einleitung in das A.T., 1969, 343, and McKane, W., Proverbs, 1970, 10 ff., for their variations. Cf. also the arrangement of the different collections by Pfeiffer, R., Die religiös-sittliche Weltanschauung des Buches der Sprüche, 1897, 5—9: Pfeiffer takes Collection C to be an addendum to Collection A.

Chapter 2: The Formal Structure of The Wisdom

2.1 Introductory Notes

For an overall view we must take note of the different genres (Gattungen) in the wisdom literature. These notes will be brief and introductory. Our aim, ultimately, is to highlight only one of these genres (Gattungen), which is the one to be discussed in detail.

As one reads through all the studies[1] written about the structure and genre of the wisdom literature, a kaleidoscopic and confusing variation in terminological usage comes to view[2].

I am convinced that it is sometimes very difficult to determine whether a certain feature within a genre (Gattung) is only a structural variation or indicative of a new genre. This problem may best be overcome by specifying the essentials of a genre in such a way as to allow for the greatest possible amount of structural variations. Too wide a classification of a genre, on the other hand, won't resolve the difficulty either. Such an untenable classification we find in the study of McKane who admits of only two genres in Proverbs, viz. the Instruction (Prov 1—9 22 17—24 22 and 31 1—9) and the Sentence (Prov 10 1—22 16 24 23—34 and 25—29)[3].

Before we discuss the specific genres, let me make a few brief observations on some aspects of the *mashal*-debate — without indulging in all aspects: It cannot really be considered as a genre itself since several genres

---

[1] Cf. Schmidt, J., Studien zur Stilistik der alttestamentlichen Spruchliteratur, 1936; Eissfeldt, O., Der Maschal im Alten Testament, 1913; Johnson, A. R., VTS 3, 1955, 162—169; Crenshaw, J. L., Wisdom in Old Testament Form Criticism (ed. J. H. Hayes), 1977, 225—264; Kaiser, O., Einleitung in das Alte Testament, 1975 (3. Aufl.), 332—365; Kayatz, C., Studien zu Prov 1—9, 1966; Gese, H., RGG, Vol. 6, 1574ff.; Zimmerli, W., ZAW 51 (1933), 177—204; Baumgartner, W., ZAW 34 (1914) 161—198; Loader, J., Polariteit in die denke van Qohelet (Diss., Pretoria), 1973, 18—31; Hermisson, H.-J., Studien zur israelitischen Spruchweisheit, 1968; Van der Weiden, W. A., Le Livre des Proverbes, BibOr 23 (1970), and Marzal, A., Gleanings from the wisdom of Mari, 1976, 4—13.

[2] But for the whole corpus of Biblical literature, systematization, providing brief descriptions of each literary type and genre, led to the development, in this century, of such a bewildering amount of new terminology, that the time is now ripe for standardization for the sake of the greatest possible consensus in terminological usage in these areas of research.

[3] McKane, W., Proverbs, 1970, 3ff.

(Gattungen) can be described as *mašal*[4]. Only the context will determine the particular genre of any *mašal*.

Early Greek literature testifies to the presence of a well-developed Philosophy. In contrats with this systematic philosophy, the Ancient Near East tends to express wisdom in the form of gnomic sayings and aphorisms[5] (which is not to say that gnomic sayings do not occur in early Greek literature — an amazing corpus exists!). This experiential knowledge of the world conceived in the form of gnomic sayings, is called *mĕšālîm* in the Old Testament. Studies roundabout the turn of this century tended, as a rule, to depend too much on etymology in determining the basic meaning of *mšl*. N. Peters even tried to derive the two-membered structure of the proverb (*mšl*) from the Assyrian *mišlu*[6]! O. Eissfeldt's criticism of this attempted derivation is quite correct[7]. W. McKane has recently emphasized the timeless and paradigmatic character of the *mashal* and therefore renders *mšl* as *paradigm, model* or *exemplar*[8]. McKane maintains that *mšl* in the Old Testament has nothing to do with »to rule«[9]. McKane maintains that *mšl* is a secondary appendage so that one may not begin with the popular proverb in order to establish the meaning of *mšl*[10]. It is an interesting attempt to broaden the description of *mšl*, but it does seem as though he has replaced previously accepted »basic meanings« of *mšl*, viz. »to compare« and »to rule« with a new one.

After Eissfeldt, the convention had more or less been to accept »to compare« or »to rule« as the »meanings« of *mšl*[11].

It seems clear that Eissfeldt laid too much emphasis on the comparative (gleich sein) character of the *mšl* as its »basic meaning«. The different characterizations of this genre (*mšl*) have all assumed this »basic meaning«. The fact that *mšl* is used as a semantic indicator for different genres, does not provide sufficient reason for concluding that the term (*mšl*) itself went through a series of developments in the actual usage of this term in different contexts. This dubious semantic treatment of words lies at the root of J. Schmidt's criticism of Eissfeldt, when Schmidt maintains that it is

---

[4] Cf. the different uses in Jer 23 28 31 29 Deut 28 37 I Sam 10 12 24 14 Prov 1—9 10 1—22 Eccl 9 17—10 20 Is 14 4 Mic 2 4 Hab 2 6—8 Ez 17 1—10 21 1—5 24 3—14 Num 23 7 24 3—24 Job 27 1 29 1 Ps 49 4 and Ps 78 2.

[5] Cf. Meyer, E., Ursprung und Anfänge des Christentums II, 1921, 38.

[6] Peters, N., Das Buch Jesus Sirach oder Ecclesiasticus, 1913, XLII ff. Cf. also Haupt, P., Koheleth oder Weltschmerz in der Bibel, 1905, 150.

[7] Eissfeldt, O. op.cit. 43 ff.

[8] McKane, W., Proverbs, 1970, 26.

[9] Ibid. 26.

[10] Ibid. 31.

[11] It even paves the way to the suggestion that the comparative character of *mšl* determines its absolute significance, cf. Volz, P., Hiob und Weisheit, 1921, 100.

impossible that *mšl* (with one basic meaning − »stehen«) can be used to characterize more than one genre without a direct link with the basic meaning[12].

It must be unambiguously clear that the different genres or poetic devices denotated by the term *mšl* in the Old Testament as well as its meaning must be established from the use of *mšl* in its context, hence it cannot be etymologically derived from a basic meaning of *mšl* or from a development of the term. When J. Schmidt defines *mšl* as: »für das praktische Leben gültige und bestehende Weisheitslehre«[13], it is a contextual interpretation of *mšl* in Prov 1 1ff. and has nothing to do with the so-called basic meaning of »stehen« connected with *mšl*.

It is therefore necessary to interpret *mšl* according to the context of usage and the specific genre into which the *mšl* is cast and not from a »basic meaning« forced into every context. So doing *mšl* may be variously interpreted in accordance with the specific context of its use[14], and can be used to characterize more than one genre (the variation in usage, mentioned above, is quite in line with this approach).

2.2 The Genres (Gattungen) of the Wisdom

2.2.1 The Parable

The parable as genre is well-attested in Old Testament form criticism[15]. It only appears in the later wisdom literature[16]. It is probably a development of the comparative element typical of the Sentence, usually in prose form.

It must be stated clearly that the comparison as such in the wisdom is not a separate genre. It can always be accommodated within the frame of the various genres and is found most frequently in the Sentence. The comparison may be considered a stylistic device, not a genre. The same is true of the metaphor. The metaphor is a stylistic device and occurs in various genres of the wisdom literature.

---

[12] Schmidt, J. op. cit. 4ff.

[13] Ibid. 5.

[14] Cf. eg. Frye, J. B., Semitics 5 (1977), 59−66, on the usage of *mšl* in the Book Job as legal methodology (the legal argument).

[15] Cf. McCartney, C. E., The Parables of the Old Testament, 1955, and Herbert, A. S., The Parable in the Old Testament, SJT 7 (1954), 180−196.

[16] Cf. Loader, J. A. op. cit. 24−26.

2.2.2   The Allegory

A close relative of the parable is the allegory, understood as an extension of the comparative element into a whole series of concrete sayings (cf. Prov 5 15–23 Eccl 12 1–6 and Amenemope VI 1–10).

It is noteworthy that the metaphor as a poetic device frequently occurs in the allegory. This has led some to a mistaken description of the allegory as but a series of combined metaphors[17].

2.2.3   The Fable

The fable does not contrast with the two genres mentioned, but is, in fact, determined by the same comparative aspect. Accordingly, elucidation, description or even criticism of human behaviour is effected by comparison with the world of animals or plants in narrative explication (cf. Judg 9 8–15).

The fable frequently occurs in the Mesopotamian wisdom literature[18], and it is reasonable to believe that this genre developed in wisdom circles as an educational form[19]. The prophets too make use of elements of the fable[20]. But the typical form of Near Eastern fable is not found in Old Testament wisdom literature.

2.2.4   The Riddle

According to 1 Kings 10 1–3 Solomon could solve all riddles put to him. According to tradition the riddle is part of wisdom. Again it is the comparison that makes the riddle possible. Without the comparative element there would be a considerable gap between question and answer — a constitutive element of the riddle[21]. Because of this very feature, one can assume a connection between popular saying and riddle in earlier stages[22] (cf. Prov 1 6 Ps 78 2 Sir 39 3 and Wisd. of Sol. 8 8).

Originally the riddle deals with the mysteries of world experience or points in the direction of hidden power. This explains the »riddle-battle« as a way to demonstrate power (cf. 1 Kings 10 1–5 and Dan 5 2). It could have played a substantial role at wedding ceremonies (cf. Judg 14 14).

---

[17] Cf. Loader, J. A. op. cit. 26.

[18] Cf. Pritchard, J. B., ANET, 592–593; Lambert, W. G., BWL, 150ff., and Gordon, E. I., JCS 12 (1958), 1–21 and 43–75. Cf. also the animal representations in the Egyptian literature and Judg 9 8–15 II Kings 14 9.

[19] Cf. Meulli, K., Herkunft und Wesen der Fabel, 1954, 65–93, and Williams, R. J., The Fable in the Ancient Near East, in: Irwin FS, 1956, 3–26.

[20] Cf. Von Rad, G., Weisheit in Israel, 1970, 65.

[21] Cf. Jolles, A., Einfache Formen, 1958, 129.

[22] Cf. Fohrer, G., Einleitung in das A. T., 1965, 339. Cf. also Torczyner, H., The Riddle in the Bible, HUCA 1 (1924), 125–149; Andrae, T., RGG² IV, 1685; Crenshaw, J. L. op. cit. 240ff. and David, Yonah, Semitics 5, 32–35.

It is impossible to maintain the view of A. Jolles[23] that the riddle does not occur within the man-world relation. The riddle is not .an isolated cognitive activity without reference to the experienced world. The question of the riddle is therefore usually a description of known experienced objects or a description of experienced behaviour (cf. Samson-riddle).

Another aspect of the riddle is the fact that it translates the paradox of reality[24] into a question-answer-system, e.g.: What is stronger than an elephant? An ant!!

Within the wisdom tradition the riddle might have had an educational function and it is a pity that so little of such a fascinating genre is left to us in the literature of the Old Testament.

2.2.5 The Numerical Saying[25]

Well-known are the numerical sayings in Prov 30 6 16–19 and Sir 25 7–11 (Prov 25 3 and 20 12 are strongly reminiscent of numerical sayings, although we find no numbers in them).

Comparison with the riddle quickly suggests that these genres are related. Torczyner even proposes the possibility that Prov 30 18–19 might originally have existed in question form (riddle form)[26].

Unlike the riddle the numerical saying stresses the amazement of discovery in life-experience and attempts to grasp its essence. The numerical sayings are reflections of the inherent will of man to systemize and order his knowledge and experience[27].

Various phenomena, to our mind sometimes contradictory, are put within a system in essential relation, or are harmonized by the conclusion deductively derived. In other words: phenomena are systematized according to a certain aspect of them or according to a certain experience of those phenomena. The use of numerical sayings is an elementary way of expressing order or of systematising results. In Biblical literature various number patterns are used to order phenomena, eg.:

1–2: Job 33 14–15 Ps 62 12 Sir 50 25–26
2–2: Prov 20 10
2–3: Job 13 20–22 Sir 26 28
3–4: (Most popular): Prov 30 15ff. 30 18ff., 30 29f. 30 21f. Cf. also
      Amos 1 and 2.

---

[23] Jolles, A. op. cit. 129.
[24] Cf. Müller, H-P., VT 20 (1970), 465–489.
[25] Cf. Stevenson, W. B., A Mnemonic Use of Numbers in Proverbs and Ben Sira, Transact. Glasgow Univ. Or. Soc. 9 (1938/39), 26–38; Buzy, D., RB 42 (1933), 5–13; Roth, W. M. W., Numerical Sayings in the Old Testament, 1965, and Hempel, J., BZAW 77, 1958, 73ff.
[26] Torczyner, H. op. cit. 135–136.
[27] Müller, H-P. op.cit. 465–489 and von Rad, G. op.cit. 53–58.

6—7: Prov 6 16–19 Job 5 19–22
9—10: Sir 25 7–11

If we examine one of these numerical sayings more closely, we find an astonishing system:

> Prov 30 18–19: There are three which are beyond my comprehension,
> four which I do not grasp:
> The *way* of an eagle in the *heavens*,
> the *way* of a snake on a *rock*
> the *way* of a ship on the *seas*
> and the *way* of a man with a *woman*.

The climax is reached in the fourth saying in the scheme 3 = 3 + 1 (4).

Notice the system by which the saying combines the three known aspects of the cosmos (heaven, earth, sea) with a human spiritual aspect.

Discovery of Ugaritic literature gave rise to the suggestion that the Biblical numerical sayings must be ascribed to Canaanite influence[28]. Attention is paid to the numerical sayings in Text 51 and the Keret-epic as proof of the Canaanite influence.

2.2.6   Onomastica

Whether this is a specific genre is disputable[29], but it is definitely a literary device of wisdom which represents the earliest scientific and encyclopaedic form of counting and ordering things. The purpose of these onomastica in the literature is not to present a scientific classification as such; instead the classification serves as premise for clarification of some matter or for ordering one's thoughts.

In 1 Kings 5 12ff. it is stated that Solomon composed 3,000 proverbs and 1,005 songs. Then it is said what all these sayings and songs are about. Evidently they represented a systematic classification of the botanic and zoological species and each of these groups are again subdivided according to the four basic types: birds, animals (land), reptiles and fish.

This classification of knowledge is well-known in the whole Ancient Near East. Not only the natural, but also the human world are categorized. This form of onomastica was the first literary form of philosophy, cosmology, chronology, astronomy, zoology, botany, demonology, medicine, etc.[30].

Comparable texts in Biblical literature are e. g. Job 24 5–8 24 14–16 28 2–8 36 27–37 13 40 15–24 40 25–41 1ff. Ps 148 and Sir 43, etc.

---

[28] Cf. Sauer, G., Die Sprüche Agurs, 1963, 116–121, and Bea, A., Bibl 21 (1940), 196–198.
[29] Crenshaw, J. L. op.cit. 245.
[30] Cf. Richter, H., ZAW 70 (1958), 1–20.

2.2.7 Wisdom Teaching (Lehrrede)

The systematic and logical combination of Sentences about a specific topic, is called a »wisdom teaching« (Lehrrede)[31]. The »Sitz im Leben« (life-setting) of his genre is the educational situation (school), and according to C. Kayatz on the Egyptian pattern[32]. This genre might even include other genres such as the Hymn (cf. Job 28 22ff. Ps 104 24ff. and Sir 24). The greater part of Prov 1−9 consists of wisdom teachings (cf. Lang and Kayatz). Psalms 49 37 and 73 might also be classified as wisdom teachings. The well-known poem on time in Eccl 3 1−8 might also be characterized as a wisdom teaching.

This genre was definitely a didactic device and occurs relatively late in Biblical literature (after the stabilization of the school).

2.2.8 The Hymn

The hymn in the wisdom literature normally plays a subordinate role within another genre, but is undeniably a genre itself. Interestingly enough these hymnic parts frequently occur in the wisdom literature when the cosmic transcendence of wisdom (hypostatization) is emphasized or when dealing with the sphere of creation (cf. especially Prov 8 22ff. Job 28 and Sir 24)[33]. C. Kayatz, over-awed by the Egyptian analogy, places undue emphasis on the Egyptian background of these hymns[34]. The hypostatization of *MAAT* in Egypt and of wisdom in Israel is enough reason for Kayatz to conclude to such an influence. If correct, a considerable number of Psalms should then be regarded as under Egyptian influence!

2.2.9 The Dialogue

Various attempts have been made to classify Job as one genre. It certainly reflects a dialogue form and this dialogue might have its »Sitz im Leben« within the frame of the scholarly discussions amongst wise men. Gese and Von Rad have rightly described this genre as a »Streitgespräch« (which is a form of the dialogue)[35]. Although lamentations play their part in Job, the whole genre cannot be classified as a lamentation (cf. Westermann, C., *Der Aufbau des Buches Hiob*, 1956, 9ff.).

---

[31] Cf. Lang, B., Die weisheitliche Lehrrede, 1972; von Rad, G. op.cit. 58ff., and Schmidt, J. op. cit. 31ff.

[32] Kayatz, C. op.cit. 135f. Cf. also Whybray, R. N., Wisdom in Proverbs, 1965, 53ff., and Anthes, R., Lebensregeln und Lebensweisheit der alten Ägypter, 1933, 8f.

[33] Kayatz, C., Einführung in die alttestamentliche Weisheit, 1969, 70−78.

[34] Cf. also Sir 42 15−43 33 39 12−35 1 1−10 10 14−18 16 18−19 16 26−17 24 18 1−7 Job 5 9−16 9 5−12 12 13−25 26 5−14 Ps 104 Wisd of Sol 6 12−20 and 7 22−8 21.

[35] Gese, H., Lehre und Wirklichkeit in der alten Weisheit, 1958, 70ff., and von Rad, G. op.cit. 267ff.

2.2.10   Confession

The confession normally is autobiographical in style and according to Crenshaw it might have served as a proof of good credentials for the head of a school[36]. The life-setting of the confession in the wisdom literature can therefore be sought in the school (cf. Sirach's invitation to the school, Sir 33 16−18 and 51 13−22).

Eccl 1 12−2 26 is also classified as a royal confession[37] and again C. Kayatz presumes an Egyptian influence[38].

2.2.11   Beatitude

The beatitude does not only occur in the prophetic literature, but also in the wisdom literature[39]. Cf. e.g. Prov 3 13 8 32−34 14 21 16 20 20 7 28 14 29 18 Eccl 10 17 Sir 14 1−2 Ps 1 1 and 112 1. This genre occurs in the earlier as well as the later wisdom literature, and it is therefore difficult to assume a prophetic influence. The life-setting of this genre might be found in the official cult.

2.2.12   The Popular Proverb

One should have begun with this genre, because it is fundamental to the genres of the wisdom literature. This genre, formed in popular parlance, with its didactic character and lofty style[40], was already an attempt to predict and order human activity under some ethical aspect or other. It was an attempt to understand and comprehend meaning in life-experience by comparing, ordering and harmonizing phenomena. The popular proverb does not always put the exact ethical consequence clearly, but to deny any reference to human behaviour in the popular proverb, is unacceptable[41]. It becomes clear that Hermisson tends to Bentzen's thesis that the popular proverb could not be the origin of the wisdom poetry,

---

[36] Crenshaw, J. L. op. cit. 258.

[37] Strangely enough this genre is classified as »King's fiction«, cf. Loader, J. A. op. cit. 19.

[38] Kayatz, C. op. cit. 47 ff. Cf. also O. Loretz' description of the so-called »Ich-Erzählung«, CBQ 25 (1963), 46−59.

[39] Kayatz, C. op. cit. 1966, 50−52.

[40] Cf. Jolles, A. op. cit. 150−151. It is very difficult to find a definition of a proverb which includes all the essential elements. It is almost an »incommµnicable quality« (according to A. Taylor, The Proverb, 1931, 3) which tells us what sentence is proverbial and which is not.

[41] Compare Hermisson, H. op. cit. 36, when he stated the essence of a popular proverb: ». . . es muß einen Schluß aus einer Summe von Erfahrungen ziehen oder auch einen Tatbestand, eine Ordnung einfach konstatieren, ohne daß damit ein Hinweis gegeben werden soll, was ein Mensch tun oder lassen sollte«.

since the wisdom poetry was literature by scholars for scholars[42]. The essence and character of the popular proverb makes such an absolute contrast quite unwarranted. Against Hermisson it must be stated that even the proverbs are not the result of school-institutions but they existed before the schools did. That does not deny the fact that the wisdom literature is used, compiled, ordered, expanded, etc. in established schools (cf. later discussion on the »life-setting«).

The popular proverb did not have to be familiar to the people as a whole: different types vary in frequency within different groups, located in different geographical areas, different families and different professional groups.

Only a small amount of real popular proverbs are to be found in Biblical literature[43] – the majority might have been collected and revitalized in the wisdom schools. Due to a relatively small amount of real popular proverbs and the interpretation of the popular proverb as a »primitive« form of the wisdom sentence, scholars jumped to the conclusion that the popular proverb was anterior to the literary proverb, and found extension and literary refinement in later stages (in official wisdom circles and schools)[44]. It is then normally suggested that this development began with the one-membered literary proverb (Kunstspruch)[45].

If we look at the number of available popular sayings there is no reason to give priority to the one-member popular proverb at the expense of the two-member sayings as if the one-member saying is the original. Form-critically it might seem logical, but if we take into consideration the meaning of the popular proverb and its relation to world experience, on the one hand, and its proclamation, of »truths« by means of comparing phenomena on the other, then it seems reasonable to accept the two-membered formulation as being as original as the one-membered proverb. The explicitly two-membered structure is often truncated through the use of the metaphor as a structural device.

It is reasonable to accept a literary refinement of a number of popular proverbs in the wisdom circles, especially with regard to a more explicit didactic character, but this does not mean a sudden fade-away of the popular proverb – both existed hand in hand.

---

[42] Hermisson, H. op. cit. 36.

[43] Cf. eg. Gen 10 9 I Sam 10 12 (dito 19 24) 1 Sam 24 14 II Sam 5 8 I Kings 20 11 Jer 13 23 23 28 31 29 Ez 16 44 18 2 Hos 4 9 Prov 1 17 11 2 13 3 Sir 10 2.

[44] Eissfeldt, O., BZAW 24, 1913, and his Einleitung in das A. T., 1964³, 109 ff. Cf. also Fohrer op. cit. 1965¹⁰, 339 ff., and Westermann, C., Weisheit im Sprichwort, in: Schalom (ed. I. H. Bernhardt), 1971, 74 and 80.

[45] Cf. Schmidt, J. op. cit. 34 ff.

2.2.13   The Sentence (»Weisheitsspruch«)

The sentence-literature forms the substantial part of the wisdom literature and is frequently (without form-critical precision) referred to as *mĕšālîm*. It is in metric form and consists mainly of a two-membered long verse as basic form (*paralellismus membrorum*).

Some scholars rejected the paralellistic character of the proverb as being its original form[46]. The *paralellismus membrorum* then would be the result of artistic hands in »academic« circles. It seems doubtful, however, since the *paralellismus membrorum* occurs as the original literary explication of oriental world experience, in which reality is described by means of two symmetric aspects of it[47]. Truth or reality is the sum of the truth/reality of the two symmetric aspects. We might say that the parallelismus is the stereometric of Oriental rational activity.

The method of handling stylistic forms of the proverb as a development from a single sentence into a two-membered sentence and eventually to a composition, sounds reasonable (form-critically), but it is not sufficient for the postulation of a linear development[48]. The occurrence of greater semantic units does not indicate an evolutionary process. The smaller and the bigger units could have existed side by side. The bigger unit is to a certain extent the repertoire of the sage on a certain topic. This assumption might evoke criticism in view of the bigger semantic units in Prov 1−9, which are obviously late (Persian Period), but it must be stated that the date is derived from the theological contents of Prov 1−9 and not only from the form[49]. It must also be stated that even in the older wisdom certain topic-units can be traced.

We therefore suggest that the two-membered proverb is original. With the development of the educational system there might have been a tendency towards greater semantic units, but no unilinear development can be attested.

The *paralellismus membrorum* as the basic structure of the proverb can be formulated synonymously[50], synthetically[51] and antithetically[52]. J. Schmidt[53], in his analysis of the Sentence literature, accepted the classifi-

---

[46] Cf. Schmidt, J. op. cit. 14 ff.

[47] Cf. the description of von Rad, G. op. cit. 42 ff. which correlates with this view.

[48] This assumption might still be the result of idealism, as developed during the »Aufklärung«, and later also influenced form-critical studies of the Bible.

[49] Cf. Kayatz, C. op. cit. 135 ff. attempts to prove a relatively early date for Prov 1−9 in comparison with the Egyptian Instruction.

[50] E.g. Prov 17 21 29 22 Job 5 18 18 5.6 Eccl 3 1 3 16 Ps 19 9 33 11 Sir 6 32 11 5 13 1 etc.

[51] E.g. Prov 7 1.2 16 31 24 22 29 24 Job 15 28 28 16 Eccl 4 9−12 Sir 4 21 17 2 18 21 42 9−10, etc.

[52] E.g. Prov 2 21 4 18 10 3 10 4 15 17.18 16 1 Job 8 20 14 21 Eccl 2 14 8 12.13 9 2 10 16.17 Sir 3 14.15.16 31 3.4, etc.

[53] Op. cit. 53 ff.

cation of R. Bultmann[54] in two categories, namely the »constitutive« and »ornamental« motives. The category of the constitutive motives consists of the wisdom saying (*Aussage*), admonition and the question. The ornamental motives, on the other hand, are the antithesis, synonym, paranomasia and the example.

Bultmann's classification is form-critically unacceptable, because it involves a dubious jumbling of genre and stylistic devices. There are only *two* basic forms in the Sentence: the wisdom saying (*Aussage*) and the wisdom admonition (*Mahnwort*)[55].

Since our aim is a detailed discussion of the wisdom admonition and its relation to the wisdom saying (*Aussage*), our remarks about the wisdom saying will be brief at this point. The best linguistic description of the wisdom saying is provided by H. Hermisson[56]. The so-called *ṭob*-proverbs are not a separate genre, but only a form-variation of the wisdom saying (*Aussage*)[57]. Classification of the beatitude (Heilspruch) is extremely difficult. We have treated it as a separate genre (see above), but in the final analysis it appears as if this genre (as well as the so-called threat), is linked with the admonition and not with the »Aussage«[58], for the preponderant accent in these sayings is on exhortation.

In the following chapter we will deal in detail with the linguistic form and interpretation of the admonition, and its relation to the wisdom saying. Hence we conclude this brief discussion of the different genres, to concentrate more specifically on the topic of this thesis.

---

[54] Bultmann, R., Die Geschichte der synoptischen Tradition, 1936 (1964[6]), 73 ff. These categories are also accepted by Richter, W., Exegese als Literaturwissenschaft, 1971, 79 ff.

[55] Cf. the erroneous treatment of the sentence as »Aussage« by Postel, J., Form and Function of the Motive Clause in Prov 10–29 (Diss. Iowa), 1976, 7–10 and 12.

[56] Op.cit. 141–174. Cf. also Schmidt, J. op.cit. 53 ff. and Zeller, D., Die weisheitlichen Mahnsprüche bei den Synoptikern, 1977, 17.

[57] Erroneously described by Loader, J. A., Polariteit in die Denke van Qohelet (Diss. Pretoria), 1973, 22–23.

[58] The prerogative of Hermisson, H.-J. op. cit. 160 ff.

Chapter 3: The Wisdom Admonition

As has been observed in Capter I, the cataloguing of the admonitions in Proverbs will be done in consideration of the connected motivative clauses, although we will pay due attention to the different exhortative formulations.

The analysis of the texts concerned, will not delve into all the intricasies of text-critical problems and interpretative assumptions advanced by the scholars who worked on these texts. To do so would take this enquiry beyond its limits and can hardly serve our declared purpose.

Only texts crucial to our purpose will be discussed in full. I am quite aware of the risk this entails. Too brief a treatment of a proverb easily makes for misunderstanding. The contents of a proverb is often of such a nature that one has to deal with it in full, so that the coherence of admonition and motivation can be understood. Our conclusions on the ethos and interpretation of the admonitions frequently require additional illustration. It is often, as will be seen, difficult to decide whether a motivation can be strictly linked to a fixed category. To that end we took the structural and the semantic aspect into consideration to determine to which group a specific admonition belongs. It is obvious that different opinions might exist, because no unanimous interpretation of the particular proverbs exists. Structural differences, on the other hand, sometimes make separate treatment necessary.

3.1 The Structure of the Admonition in Proverbs

At the end of his chapter (par 3.2.1) an index of the various texts discussed is given together with their essential grammatical and syntactical features.

Apart from the regular sequence of admonition-motivation, attention is also given to those admonitions in which the motivation appears as a secondary command, to those in which the motivation precedes the imperative form of the admonition and to those admonitions that occur in complex structures, e.g. in Prov 1–9.

3.1.1 Admonition – Motivation in a Final Clause

Let us begin by paying attention to two admonitions (Prov 22:6 and 16 3) in which the motivation in the final clause might possibly be described as an asyndetic subordinate clause. We, however, maintain the broader classification of the final clause, because it offers better scope for the description of the semantic bearance.

Prov 16 3

gó̄l(gal) ʿɛl-yhwh maʿăśêkā
wĕyikkōnû maḥšĕbōtêkā
Reveal your doing to the Lord,
so that your plans might be fulfilled.

The function of the motivation in the *wĕyiqtōl*-form is to express the ultimate consequence of the admonition in 3a. According to the paradigma of the older wisdom, v. 3b is not promissory in character[1], but a statement of factual truth, on condition of obedience to the admonition in 3a. The relation to Jahweh in the nature and manner of one's doing determines the actual worth of it. Fulfillment of the plans can only be achieved when one's acts correspond with the fixed created order through recognition of the Lord of this order (cf. Prov 16 1–2).

Noteworthy is the fact that the first two wisdom sayings in Prov 16 reflect the same topic as v. 3 and must therefore be treated as part of the motivation for the admonition in 3a. That is why 3b is put in a final clause as the motivative climax.

Although these three verses dwell on the same topic, the admonition makes the ethical demand explicit. The admonition further makes the educative goal evident − in a more pregnant sense than does the wisdom saying (Aussage).

Prov 22 6

ḥănōk lannaʿar ʿal-pî darkô
gam kî-yazqîn lô-yāsûr mimmɛnnâ
Educate a boy according to the requirements of his way[2]
so that even in old age he will not leave it.

Postel presumes that the intention of the admonition is to educate a youth according to his potential and ability[3]. It is not totally excluded, but the motivation makes it evident that the importance lies in the education according to the requirements of his *drk* − that means the normative way of living. This admonition gives direction to the educational process. When the education meets the requirements of the responsible living (orderly living), then in old age the boy will have good foundation to follow the right way[4].

---

[1] Cf. Postel, J. op. cit. 40.
[2] A dynamic equivalent of *ʿal-pî darkô*.
[3] Postel, J. op. cit. 52−53.
[4] Cf. McKane, W. op. cit. 564 and Scott, R.B.Y., Proverbs. Ecclesiastes, 1965, 127.

W. Richter characterises v. 6b as a conditional sentence[5]. The two co-ordinative clauses in v. 6b reflect a conditional relation, but the relation of the motivation in v. 6b and the admonition in v. 6a cannot be described as conditional — v. 6b is a final clause with regard to v. 6a. The admonition is positively formulated, connected with the final consequence as motivation.

Prov. 22 10

gārēš lēṣ wĕyēṣēʾmādôn
wĕyišbōt dîn wĕqālôn
Drive out a scoffer[6], then strife goes out,
litigation and insult also cease.

At first sight it seems as if the poetic parallelism is forced into this proverb — reflected in a double motivation in v. 10aβ and 10b, both introduced with *wĕ-*. But if we look at the climactic arrangement of the three nouns *mādôn, dîn* and *qālôn* (the latter as the utmost of inhuman behaviour in this respect), we have in fact semantically only one motivation.

Prov 9 9a + 9 9b

tēn lĕḥākām wĕyɛḥkām-ʿôd
hôdaʿ lĕṣaddîq wĕyôsɛp lɛqaḥ
Instruct the wise, and even wiser he will be;
Inform the righteous man and he will increase understanding.

In both these two admonitions the motivative clauses (*wĕ* + Impf) linguistically seem to be instances of ordinary co-ordination. They are however factual statements about the final consequence of the prescribed behaviour in the admonitions (v. 9aα and 9bα).

Here we have one of the shortest forms of an admonition accompanied, evidently, by a motivation.

Verses 7–12 plainly interrupt the poem of Chapter 9 about the invitation of the wise and foolish woman[7]. Furthermore, v. 7—v. 9 reflect the attitude of the older wisdom with its causal linkage of event-consequence. All the more reason to consider the motivative clauses to be final and not conditional clauses[8].

---

[5] Richter, W. op. cit. 41.

[6] From this proverb it is also clear that the *lēṣ* in Proverbs is not the ordinary mocker, but the obstinate and trouble-seeking person — the opposite of the wise.

[7] Compare the translation of McKane, W. op. cit. 224: »Give instruction to a wise man *that he may be* wiser still, inform a righteous man *that he may* increase his learning.«

[8] It is hard to say according to which principles such a literary collection came into being. It is clear, even in the Collections B. and E., that they are not a mere arbitrary arrangement of proverbs, but certain »methods« must have been followed. With regard to our passage: Did the polarization of the wise and the foolish in the form of poetic personification make it possible to introduce »traditional« proverbs on this theme in-between? Verses 7–11 are therefore not irrelevant in this context. Or, did the »editor« insert a piece of the wise-

Prov 19 20

šĕmaʿ ʿēṣâ wĕqabbēl mûsār
lĕmaʿan tɛḥkam bĕʾaḥărîtɛkā
Listen to advice and accept instruction
that you may be wise in future.

The translation of the motivative clause by McKane[9] is not acceptable. Although semantically plausible, a lot of linguistic problems are raised if one inverts the sentence so that the ʾaḥărît becomes the subject. The author does not characterize the »end« of a wise person, but he lays emphasis on the »career« of the pupil who listens to advice and instruction. It does not mean that after a process the pupil will in the end be wise: No, he must accept advice, etc. so that his future (after being confrontated with mûsār and ʿēṣâ) may be wise[10].

It seems a case of circular reasoning when McKane forces ʾaḥărît into the meaning of »life«[11] which in the final analysis implies just what he seeks to deny.

Noteworthy is the fact that the admonition with two imperatives is followed by only one motivation in a final clause, introduced by lĕmaʿan.

Prov 22 24–25

ʾal-titraʿ ʾɛt-baʿal ʾāp
wĕʾɛt-ʾîs ḥēmôt lōʾtābôʾ
pɛn-tɛʾlap ʾōrĕḥōtāw
wĕlāqaḥtâ môqēš lĕnapšɛkā[12]
Do not take a hot-tempered man for a friend
and do not keep company with a hothead;
lest you become familiar with his paths,
and alight on a lethal snare[13].

The sequence of words (viz. the nouns and verbs in the pattern a b b a) in v. 24 forms a typical chiasm. Increased effect is not only achieved by ʾîš ḥēmôt (v. 24b) (cf. baʿal ʾāp in v. 24a), but also (probably more so) by the usage of the Prohibitive in v. 24b (cf. the Vetitive in v. 24a). The occurrence of the lōʾ-form in v. 24b in this almost synonymic parallelism, must be defined like the ʾal-form in v. 24a. It is a mere stylistic device and it is

---

foolish polarization proper to a new frame of theological interpretation of wisdom? Especially v. 11 might be such a new interpretation − in Deuteronomistic style! Particularly in view of Chapter 9's theme, the invitation of wisdom, it would seem that the author intended to make the theological understanding of wisdom clear. Whatever the position, v. 7–11 is not irrelevant singly because it is an intersection.

9 McKane, W. op. cit. 240 and 524.
10 Cf. Prov 15 32.
11 McKane, W. op. cit. 524.
12 Cf. ANET 423 for the Amenemope parallel.
13 Translation of McKane, W. op. cit. 245−246.

impossible to seek different settings in life for these two admonitions. We must therefore be careful not to overestimate the importance of the Prohibitive on behalf of the Vetitive in the wisdom admonitions.

It is of importance for our eventual interpretation of wisdom's ethos to take note of the fact that it is the *baʿal ʾāp* and the *ʾîš ḥēmôt* who violate orderly human existence through injurious acts. Self-destruction is the outcome of such behaviour.

> *Prov 25 8*
>
> *ʾăšer rāʾû ʿênêkā ʾal-tēṣēʾ lārib mahēr*
> *pɛn mah-taʿăśɛh beʾaḥărîtāh bĕhaklîm ʾōtĕkā rēʿɛkā*[14]
> Do not hastily take to court what your eyes have seen,
>   what will you do afterwards if your neighbour brings disgrace upon you?

According to MT. v. 7c is attached to the preceding v. 7. The metric structure requires that v. 7c be interpreted within the context of v. 8, not v. 7. Semantically the whole context reflects the well-known moral attitude of reticence in the wisdom of the Ancient Near East. The admonition in v. 8 without 7c would be vague and unconditional. Logically v. 7c, attached to v. 7, makes no sense and would seem to limit the motivation of v. 7.

McKane and others (Toy, Gemser, etc.) deny the legal setting of this saying, because it is directed against »indiscreet and injurious gossip«[15]. This interpretation rests mainly on the textual emendation of the MT:

> *tēṣēʾ − tōṣēʾ*
> and
> *lārib − lārōb*[16].

Although we cannot deny some reference to injurious gossip, the motive clause makes a forensic setting of this saying indisputable. An eye-witness' testimony, if inaccurate, might be repudiated in court and the innocent defendant might even prosecute the accuser.

Formally the motivation in v. 8b ought to be discussed under the category of motivations introduced by an interrogative clause, but I treat it as a final clause in which the final result of the behaviour in the admonition of v. 8a is described in the form of a question. Noteworthy is the maintenance of the *pɛn*[17] before *mah* as indication of its final purpose.

> *Prov 26 4−5*
>
> 4 *ʾal-taʿan kĕsîl kĕʾiwwaltô*
> *pɛn-tišwēh-lô gam-ʾāttâ*

---

[14] Cf. Amenemope XXII:11ff.

[15] McKane, W. op. cit. 580. Cf. also Toy, C. H., The Book of Proverbs, 1959, 460.

[16] Cf. the translation of Symmachus in which these words are respectively translated with ἐξενέγκῃς and εἰς πλῆθος.

[17] Not necessary to read *kî* instead of *pɛn*.

5 ʿanēh kĕsîl kĕʾiwwaltô
   pɛn yihyɛh ḥākām bĕʿênâw

4 Answer not a fool according to his folly,
   lest you yourself also become like unto him.
5 Answer the fool according to his folly,
   lest he regard himself as wise.

It seems contradictory to find a negative admonition in v. 4 and a positive one in v. 5 concerning one and the same person (kĕsîl).

Here we meet an aspect of oriental logic — truth is not a merely inductive process of harmonizing, but experiential truth must be maintained even if it requires paradox. The truth of a phenomenon or behaviour is the entirety of the two aspects of its polarity (or symmetry)[18]. Thus to be true to the conduct of the kĕsîl, the opposite of the ḥākām and the ṣaddîq, both admonitions in v. 4 and v. 5 must be maintained. Truth is not to keep quiet when a fool talks nonsense, for that would reduce you to his level (cf. v. 4b); the fool might keep on talking (in spite of the wise man's silence) and give advice in a self-conceited manner, proclaiming he is the wise. Such a self-assertive fool is even worse (cf. v. 5b), and he should be shaken loose from his illusions and be exposed in his real position. In v. 4 emphasis is laid on the recognition of the questions of the fool as if they were justifiable questions and in v. 5 account is given of the wise answer which exposes the illusions of the fool[19]. In this regard we may recall Prov 15 23:

»A man gets pleasure from an apt answer
And how good is a well-timed word!«

V. 5 is not put in by a sage who was opposed to the truth of v. 4[20]. This view simply lacks the perspective of the symmetry of sayings.

Both motivations consists of a final clause, introduced by pɛn.

Only one more example of an admonition with its motive clause introduced by pɛn will be discussed, namely Prov 5 7–14. We omit quotation from the Hebrew text, for it entails few text-critical problems. The chief one is the use of the plural in the first admonition (v. 7) and of the singular in the second (v. 8). It is, however, not necessary to emendate the text, for v. 7 is, so to speak, the »terminus technicus« or general introduction of the wisdom teacher, calling for attention. The specific teaching starts with v. 8, which is more individually directed, and therefore in the singular.

---

[18] It is therefore incorrect to evaluate these two sayings as absurd (Zimmerli, W. op. cit. 187f.) if the authority of both admonitions is maintained. The major concern of these two admonitions is not to indicate the »rechten Mittelweg zwischen Anpassung und Distanz« (Skladny, U. op. cit. 51).
[19] Cf. Delitzsch, F., Biblical Commentary on the Proverbs of Solomon, II 1872, 175–176.
[20] Gordis, R., JQR 30 (1939), 137.

The admonition consists literally of two admonitions (v. 7+8), each containing both a positive and a negative demand. It deserves notice that the admonition is semantically and linguistically linked to the preceding predication of the *zārâ* (cf. v. 3). The direct motivation for this admonition follows in v. 9–14 and is introduced by *pɛn*. The motivation (v. 9–14) puts forward a description of the final end by means of a sequence of negative consequences, in case the »strange« woman is not avoided.

It needs saying that there is no direct motivation in the first admonition in v. 7. From the structure, however, it becomes clear that the admonition against the *zārâ* and its direct admonition (v. 9–11) are embedded within the first admonition (v. 7) and its motivation (v. 12–14). But we cannot make a separation between v. 11 and v. 12, because the first admonition and its motivation, for their validity, depend upon the second admonition. So, we find a poetically cross-linked motivation in the form of a circular structure:

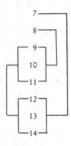

The vertical lines on the right in this diagram indicate the relation of admonition and motivation (each 3 verses). The vertical lines on the left indicate that no separation can be made between v. 11 and v. 12, for both motivations are cross-linked[21].

The following admonitions are followed by motivations in final clauses, introduced by *pɛn*: Prov 25 9–10 25 16 25 17 30 10 30 8–9 31 4–5 and 9 8a. Although these admonitions are not discussed in full, the peculiarities of these sayings will be considered in our conclusive remarks. We now proceed to 2 (3?) cases in which the motivation in a final clause is introduced by the preposition *lĕ*:

Prov 5 1–2

In v. 1 we get a positive admonition with two Imperatives. In v. 2 we find the first direct motivation in the form of a final clause, which expresses the final purpose of obedience to wisdom teaching. Some will immediately observe that the motivation starts in v. 3. That is correct, but v. 2 which puts

---

[21] As will be seen later, these interesting and complex structures mainly occur in the later wisdom literature of Prov 1–9.

forward the reasons for listening to wisdom, forms part of the motivation and forms the transition to the predication of the *zārâ* as final motivation. The function of v. 2 is not promissory. At a later stage (motivations as predications) we will return in full to Prov 5 1–6 for a more complete discussion of it and the crucial role of the *zārâ* in this respect.

Prov 7 1–5

We find more or less the same structure in this passage. In the first four verses there are eight commands, stated positively (6) or negatively (2). The motivation follows in v. 5 in the form of a final clause, introduced by *lě* + *Inf Cstr*, which describes the reason for obeying wisdom teaching. As in Chapter 5, v. 5 of Chapter 7 is followed by a secondary motivation in the form of a predication of the *zārâ* (already mentioned in v. 5). Why the predication of the *zārâ* so often follows the injunction to obey wisdom teaching, will be discussed at a later stage (cf. previous remark about Chapter 5 1–6).

Of interest is the occurrence of a secondary motivation in v. 2aβ. It follows directly upon the admonition to keep the commandments. The motivation is in the form of a promise and reflects Deuteronomistic influence with its typical promise of life on condition of obedience of the law-stipulations.

> *Prov 22 20–21*
> 20 *hălô' kātabtî lěkā šāliwi(w)m (MT) běmô'ęṣ̂ôt wādā'at*
> 21 *lěhôdî'ăkā qōšṭ 'imrê 'ěmɛt*
>   *lěhāšîb 'ămārîm 'ěmɛt lěšōlěhêkā*
> Didn't I write out for you thirty sayings *with knowledge* to impart to you truth and truthful words and wise advice,
> that you may take back a true report to him who sends you.

Without going into all the text-critical problems concerning v. 20 (so crucial in the discussion of the relation of Amenemope and Prov 22 17–24 22), we will restrict ourselves to the question whether v. 20 could be treated as an admonition. Structurally there is no imperative saying, but on the other hand it is difficult to formulate an admonition in the first person. Verse 20 could have been formulated positively, but then clearly we could not recognize a demand. Isn't it possible therefore that the negative style with *hălô'* is used to express a sort of admonition or exhortation? In English this negative usage is well-known: e. g. Didn't I tell you to stop reading, you'll miss the train! The semantic effect is the same as: Stop reading! Interestingly enough the motivation follows more or less the same structure as that of Prov 5 1–2 and 7 1–5: v. 21a expresses the purpose and v. 21b the motivation in the form of a final clause, introduced by the preposition *lě* + *Inf Cstr*.

I am therefore inclined to suggest that the use of the interrogative *hălô'* in the wisdom literature is a form of admonition.

Prov 19 27

MT. *ḥădal-běnî lišmōa' mûsār*
   lišgôt mē'imrê-dā'at
   A son who ceases to attend to discipline,
   strays from teaching of knowledge.

According to the MT v. 27 consists of an admonition (in Imperative form) followed by a motivation in a final clause.

It is, however, problematic to accept the Imperative form of *ḥdl* in v. 27 — that would certainly express the opposite of what is really intended. The negative polarisation of *mûsār* and *'imrê-dā'at* is unknown and the treatment of such an admonition in Coll. B (Chapter 10—22 16) is strange.

If the Imperative is accepted, there can be no reason for an Imperative in a conditional clause[22]. The only way out is to interpret the Imperative as a rhetorical device, and for its interpretation one has to accept an ironical use of certain features[23].

The LXX reading suits the context best. It would therefore be better to emendate the Imperative *ḥădal* according to the Participle (*ḥādēl*) reading of the LXX. The *Maqqef* with the Participle corresponds well with v. 26, whereas it is almost impossible with the Imperative followed by the indirect object. One could assume that the Imperative vocalization of *ḥdl* in the MT is probably due to the error of *běnî* instead of *bēn* (or vice versa). What the circumstances might be, the reading of *běnî* cannot be accepted in this context, (cf. v. 25 *lēṣ*, v. 26 *'āb* and *'ēm*, v. 27 *bēn*, etc.). One would then translate: »A son who ceases to attend to discipline, strays from teaching of knowledge.« Neglecting the acceptance of the *mûsār* also entails ignoring the teachings of knowledge.

Prov 19 27 is therefore no real admonition. For the sake of completeness, finally, I merely mention the following admonition: Prov 24 17—18.

3.1.2   Admonition: Motivation in Subordinate Clause

The motivation occurs in an ordinary Subordinate clause in just these few cases: two in Coll. H and one in Coll. B.

Prov 31 3

'al-tittēn lannāšîm ḥêlekā
ûděrākêkā lamḥôt mělākîm
Give not your strength to women,
nor your »potential« to those who destroy kings.

---

[22] Gemser, B. op. cit. 77.
[23] Cf. Postel, J. op. cit. 45—47; McKane, W. op. cit. 525; Gemser, B. op. cit. 77, and Toy, C.H. op. cit. 381.

Structurally it looks like an ordinary synthetic parallelism, introduced by an admonition. In fact, 3b is also an admonition. Through verb-deletion the repetition of the verb (*ntn*) is avoided.

However, the admonition in 3a is clear, but what about the motivation which seems to be absent?

It is obvious that *děrākêkā* is the parallel of *ḥêlɛkā*. BH and Gemser suggest the emendation to *yěrēkêkā* (your loins). There is so little reason to correct *děrākêkā* that I would stick to the MT and translate *drk* in a more dynamic way[24].

The motivation consists of an ordinary subordinate clause, introduced by *wě*. The admonition stresses the danger of expending one's strength on women. The predication (in a subordinate command) of these women as those who destroy kings, is enough reason to accept v. 3b as a motivation.

Prov 31 6–7

6 *těnû šēkār lɛ°ôbēd wěyayin lěmārê nāpɛš*
7 *yištɛh wěyiškaḥ rîšô wa°ămālô lô yizkār-°ôd*
   Give liquor to a man who is in extremity
   and wine to those who feel miserable.
   That he may drink and forget his poverty
   and no more remember his troubles.

In contrast with v. 4 and 5, v. 6–7 emphasize the »healing« character of wine. Again the symmetric build-up of these sayings becomes clear: The truth about winedrinking is not exhausted by its prohibition for kings, but includes also in its commendability for people in various dispositions. The motivation (v. 7) refers to the medical and psychological effect of wine and alcohol on people in the conditions mentioned.

Prov 19 25

lēṣ takkɛh ûpɛtî ya°rim
wěhôkîaḥ lěnābôn yābîn dā°at
   Beat a scoffer and an uneducated child learns prudence,
   reprove a sensible man (and) he will gain knowledge for himself.

At first sight only one admonition occurs in v. 25b with the Imperative of *ykḥ*. Considering the context and the antithetic structure of this saying one must interpret *takkɛh* as a Jussive and not as an Imperfect. Thus, there are two admonitions, each with its own motive clause, in an antithetic pattern.

It is difficult to be exact about the character of this motivation, for it largely depends on the interpretation of it. I suggest it is an ordinary subordination. Notice the complete absence of an item between the admonition and the motivation in v. 25b; this strengthens the likelihood of subordination.

The function of the motivation is not promissory as Postel assumes[25].
It is rather a description of the final outcome when read in terms of the
traditional causal reasoning in the wisdom.

Here we have two ways of teaching, (*nkḥ* and *ykḥ*), each with different
results. Distinction is not only made in the method of teaching, but also
(and it appears to be the most important) in the result of the different
methods for various people.

The *pɛtî* learns through the example — when he sees the result of the
lēṣ-behaviour, it forces him to avoid the result and so he grows in
prudence[26]. It is the *pɛtî* (the untutored or uneducated person) who benefits
from the punishment of the foolish (*lēṣ*). There is no improvement whatsoever for the *lēṣ* himself. This view can only be understood against the
background of the older wisdom in which the *lēṣ* forms the absolute
opposite of the wise and the righteous man. The *lēṣ* and the *ḥākām* (and
ṣaddîq) are diametrically opposed to one another. In the eyes of the wise
man there is no hope for nor basis for associating with the *lēṣ*.

The effect (result) of the reproof of the *nābôn* (the sensible and intelli-
gent man)[27] is different — it leads to an understanding and knowledge of
reality: accessible only to the wise! To the *nābôn* the order of reality
becomes revealed through reproof.

The *bîn dāʿat* never occurs with the *pɛtî*. We therefore accepted that
the people intended here were classified according to competence. This
classification may have originated in the school or other educational institutions.

3.1.3   Admonition: Motivation in Result Clause or Result Description

Prov 19 18a

yassēr binkā kî-yeš tiqwâ
The NEB translates as follows: »Chastise your son while there is hope (for him).«

It depends on the interpretation of *kî-yeš*: if one interprets *kî-yeš* in a
more temporal sense, the translation would tend towards that of the NEB
proposal. It should not, however, be interpreted as a causal clause. The
result of the chastisement is the hope left for the child. It would therefore
be more satisfactory to alter the translation of the NEB as follows: Chastise
your son for then there is hope (for him). Such an interpretation suits the
context best, especially with regard to the connecting admonition in

---

[24] Cf. Bauer, J.B., VT 8 (1958), 91 ff., on his discussion of *drk* in Prov 8 22 and its possible
relation to the Ugaritic *drkt*.

[25] Postel, J. op. cit. 45.

[26] *pɛtî* is always connected with *ʿrm* in the wisdom literature. Cf. eg. Prov 1 4 and 8 5.

[27] Cf. Prov 14 6 15 14 and 18 15.

v. 18(b): Chastise, but do not go to the utmost of killing (such a temper is delayed in v. 19).

Prov 27 11

ḥăkam bĕnî wĕśammaḥ libbî
wĕʾāšîbâ ḥōrĕpî dābār
Be wise my son, and make me happy,
that I may answer my contemner.

The structure of this admonition is more or less the same as that of Prov 19 18a. The result clause is expressed in the form of a wish, with *wĕ* + *Cohortative*.

This admonition differs to some extent from the general pattern in as far as the result (in the motivation) does not effect the son himself who is wise, but the teacher. It might be because of this peculiarity that the LXX-translator came to this translation:

». . . And turn away reproachful words from yourself.«

It is not necessary to emendate the MT, for references in Prov 15 20. 23 15–16 and 29 3a are enough to establish the right understanding.

Prov 24 19–20[28]

ʾal-tithar bammĕrēʿîm
ʾal-tĕqannēʾ bārĕšāʿîm
kî lô-tihyɛh ʾaḥărît lārāʿ
nēr rĕšāʿîm yidʿāk
Do not annoy yourself about evil-doers
nor be envious of the wicked men;
For there is no future for the evil man,
the lamp of the wicked will go out.

The admonition consists of two Vetitives and the motivation is introduced by *kî*. We prefer to characterize the motivation, introduced by *kî*, in this saying and the one to be discussed next, as *Result-descriptions*. Others are content to treat them as ordinary causal clauses. Linguistically this cannot be proven incorrect, beyond a doubt, but if we (e.g.) compare this proverb with a proverb with more or less the same structure, (its motivation also introduced by *kî* as in Prov 24 1–2), it is found that semantic differences occur that must be considered. In 24 2 the very reason is stated for the truth of the admonition, but in 24 20 the reason is explicated in the form of a result-description (cf. Prov 13 9 and Job 8 5). The admonition of 20 19 is motivated with a description of the result of the behaviour of the wicked and the evil men, whereas in 24 1 the admonition is motivated by laying emphasis on the reason why one should not be envious of evil men and long for their company (cf. also 23 17–18). Initially one may

---

[28] Cf. also Prov 24 15–16 with the same structure.

be inclined to centre these admonitions' credibility and authority in the institution for lack of any mention of specific authority or directly stated reason for personal obedience in this type of motivation. However, the authority of the admonition in 24 19 does not centre in any kind of institution or person, but in the truth of the observation, as advanced by the motivation (24 20)[29].

> *Prov 24 21–22*
>
> *yĕrā'-'ɛt-yhwh bĕnî wāmɛlɛk*
> *'im-šônîm 'al-tit'ārāb*
> *kî-pit'ōm yāqûm 'ēdām*
> *ûpîd šĕnêhɛm mî yôdēaʿ*
>
> Fear Jahweh and the king, my son,
> do not consort with the rebellious;
> for their misfortune will come suddenly
> and who will notice the decay of their years (life).

The well-nigh universally accepted translation of *šônîm* as noblemen[30], is unacceptable. *Šônîm* is the Particle of *šnh* and could be translated by *those who change, those who destroy* or a dynamic equivalent translation might even be *those who are rebellious*. It is therefore not necessary to emend the text according to the LXX-translation: καὶ μηθετερῳ αὐτῶν ἀπειθησῃς (»do not be rebellious against either of them«).

According to Gemser the motivation reflects the anger and behaviour of the king[31], but McKane maintains a reference to the retributive power of Yahweh[32].

Reference to the fear of God and the king in the admonition of v. 21 is made because God, and in a secondary sense the king, is the author of world order and cosmic harmony. They are the patrons of this order, the king (in human respect) representing the human authority for its protection. The rebellious act (of the *šônîm*) therefore means disruption of this order. The intention of the admonition is the recognition of both Jahweh and the king as guardians of the order. The motivation clearly stresses that acts of violation against the created order end in self-destruction. Rebellious acts against the king as representative of the world order, means violation of the order itself, and leads to disastrous consequences for those who commit these deeds. They will experience the severest misfortune that could be brought upon a person: They will decay without being noticed by anyone.

---

[29] The authority of the wisdom admonitions will be discussed in full later.

[30] Cf. Kopf, L., VT 9 (1959) 280; D. Winton Thomas, ZAW 52 (1934), 237 and McKane, W. op. cit. 249.

[31] Gemser, B. op. cit. 89.

[32] McKane, W. op. cit. 406. Toy, C. H. op. cit. 450 correctly maintains the supreme authority of Jahweh and the authority of the king!

It is clear that the motivation must be understood as a result-description of those people mentioned in v. 21 aβ. Without the mentioning of God and the king in v. 21 aα the saying would be totally unintelligible.

Prov 24 11–12

haṣṣēl lĕquḥîm lammāwɛt
ûmāṭîm laḥɛrɛg ʾim-taḥśôk
kî-tōʾmar hēn lōʾ-yādaʿnû zɛ̂
hălōʾtōkēn libbôt hûʾ-yābîn
wĕnōzēr napšĕkā hûʾyēdāʿ
wĕhēšîb lĕʾādām kĕpoʿŏlô
Rescue prisoners from death
and stay not away[33] from those who are led away
to be slain[34],
for if you say: Look, we know nothing about this!
he who watches over you know it and repay
everybody according to his doing[35].

One must admit that this admonition sounds strange to one's ear. This admonition calls upon people to support those imprisoned and awaiting execution. The question concerning the degree of guilt or innocence of the referred people is not mentioned. In view of the accompanying motivation, one is inclined to think of innocent people who are prosecuted unjustly, for the motivation refers to the deliberate neglect of duty, of which the all-knowing God is aware of, and for which there is no excuse. The reference to the supreme Justice who never errs in his verdict, compels us to think of innocent people. Solidarity with the wicked in their execution is inconceivable within the framework of the older wisdom[36].

The result-description of v. 12 intends to impress those who could have done something for the unjustly imprisoned, of God's justice.

Prov 23 19–21 and Prov 23 12–14

These admonitions are of basically the same structure, so that a few remarks, without their literal quotation, may suffice for our purpose.

---

[33] According to a text-critical emendation which reads *ʾal* instead of *ʾim* and *taḥsîk* instead of *taḥsôk*. There is however, insufficient grounds for accepting *ʾim* as an emphatic particle as Driver, Biblica 32, 188, does.

[34] The translation reflects the acceptance of Driver's proposal, ZAW 50 (1932), 146. Cf. also the translation of B. Gemser op. cit. 88.

[35] The interrogative particle *hă-* is considered to affect v. 12 aβ as well as v. 12b; otherwise it is difficult to explain the function of the *wĕ* in v. 12b.

[36] It is highly questionable to conclude that in wisdom circles an attitude against death as punishment for crime is to be found; cf. Delitzsch, F. op. cit. 132.

In both cases the admonition (v. 19 and v. 12) begins with a general call of obedience to the teacher on the part of the pupil (in v. 12–14 it might be the father of children). This general admonition is then particularised with a concrete prohibition (cf. v. 12 and v. 20). We find the same structure in Prov 5 7–14 and 7 24–27. The motivations, in the form of result-descriptions, are in both cases introduced by *kî* + *VS* (cf. v. 13b and v. 21). Diagrammatically the relation of the verses to one another may be represented thus:

v. 12	(v. 19)
v. 13 a	(v. 20)
v. 13 b–14	(v. 21)

The motivation follows the secondary admonition, but both are embedded within the framework of the first admonition.

Finally, a remark on Prov 23 12–14. It tells us that the lack of discipline means the death of a son/pupil. The reference here is not to physical death, but to existence in contrast to the reality of life as promised for those who obey the wisdom teaching. Evidently, the categories of life and death play an integral part in the wisdom sayings. It is, therefore, to be doubted whether the promise of life, connected with the obedience to wisdom teaching, is the result of the identification of wisdom and law. One would rather suggest that the promise of life plays an integral role in both wisdom and law, which even facilitates the eventual identification.

Prov 23 10–11

'al-tasseg gĕbûl 'ôlām
ûbiśdê yĕtômîm 'al-tābō'
kî-gō'ălām ḥāzāq
hû'-yārîb 'et-rîbām 'ittāk
Do not remove the ancient boundary stones
nor intrude on the lands of orphans,
For their redeemer is powerful,
He will fight their case with you.

The admonition occurs in a double Vetitive form and the motivation (v. 11) is a result-description, introduced with *kî* + *VS*.

The reading of the *gĕbûl 'almānâ*[37] instead of *gĕbûl 'ôlām* (MT) is hardly convincing for the lack of evidence. *gĕbûl 'almānâ* does occur in Prov 15 25, but that does not mean that it is also meant in a hendiadys pattern with *yetômîm* in Prov 23 10. Although the reference in Amenemope (Chapter 6) strengthens a reading of *gĕbûl 'almānâ*, the form *gĕbûl 'ôlām* also occurs in Prov 22 28. The admonition is quite intelligible with *gĕbûl 'ôlām*. The reference in v. 10b to the orphan, creates the framework in which the admonition, warning against the removal of boundary markers,

---

[37] Cf. Gemser, B. op. cit. 86–87 and Toy, C. H. op. cit. 431.

is to be understood. This admonition is meant to protect the rights of the underprivileged or those people in society whose rights are easily violated by the greedy people. In Ancient Near Eastern society the boundary markers are evaluated as of vital importance. The correctness of the commercial scale is viewed in due respect. They are instruments through which order and righteousness are upheld. God authorizes this order and therefore He hates false weights and the violation of legal rights by means of the removal of boundary stones. The qualification of the boundary stones as ʿôlām reflects the tradition of the land division together with the temporal fusion of individual and property. God maintains this order and therefore He will act as the redeemer or as the patron of those whose rights are violated.

The motivation describes the result of the behaviour mentioned in v. 10: The powerful God will take up the case of the underprivileged[38]!

Prov 25 6–7

The admonition consists of two Vetitive forms and the motivation begins with kî + VS as a result-description. It was said earlier that we have to interpret v. 7c in connection with v. 8[39] (according to the Vulgate). The ʾatnaḥ following nādîb strengthens this reading.

Accent is laid on humility in the presence of the mighty (to respect the right order); otherwise he who exalted himself in the midst of the mighty might be humiliated.

Prov 8 32

wĕʿattâ bānîm šimʿû-lî
wĕʿašrê dĕrākay yišmōrû[40]
And now, (my) sons, listen to me;
Happy are they who keep my ways!

This admonition's predication of the transcendence of wisdom (8 22–31) is in fact an integral part of the whole of Chapter 8, and the call of the wisdom in v. 32ff. is clearly reminiscent of the call of wisdom in 8 4ff. The whole of Chapter 8 is a poetic unity and an artistic creation in form and content beyond compare.

It is of interest that the beatitude in v. 32b clearly takes the form of a motivation[41]. It is classified as a result-description, because reference is

---

[38] God frequently appears as patron of the rights of the underprivileged in wisdom and juridical literature of the Ancient Near East; cf. eg. Fensham, F.C., JNES 21 (1962), 129–139; AION 31 (1971), 160, and my JNSL 5 (1977), 53 ff. Cf. also Bernhardt, K.-H., VTS 8 (1961), 85 f.

[39] Cf. p. 32.

[40] We maintain the reading of the MT, because the correctness of the LXX-reading cannot be verified beyond doubt.

[41] Cf. Delitzsch, F. op. cit. 194.

made to the consequence for those who have listened and kept the counsel of wisdom. The *waw* in v. 32b would therefore be significant as an assertive particle.

Prov 8 33–36

That v. 32 and v. 4ff. in Chapter 8 cohere, was indicated above. Verse 33 too refers to v. 10 of Chapter 8. The climax of Chapter 8 is not only achieved by recalling the invitation of wisdom, but especially by the accumulative development of thought in the motivative clauses.

The motivation in v. 34–36, as a result-description picturing the absolute consequences of finding or losing wisdom, forms the climax of this passage. We consider v. 35 (introduced by *kî*) not as a result clause, for no attention is paid to the reason for disobedience to wisdom-counsel, but, instead, the results for those who have or have not listened to wisdom-counsel are stressed. The direct motivation is found in v. 35 which is antithetically increased by v. 36.

Consideration has been given to v. 34–36 as the motivation for the admonition in v. 33. The direct motivation starts in v. 35, as stated above, but the beatitude cannot be isolated from the motivation and must be treated as an implicit motivation. Being a secondary motivation, v. 34 is best understood as part of the result-description.

Finally, one more example requires our attention, viz. *Prov 23 17–18*[42]:

> *ʾal-yĕqannēʾ libbĕkā baḥaṭṭāʾîm*
> *kî ʾim-bĕyirʾat-yhwh kol-hayyôm*
> *kî ʾim-yeš ʾaḥărît*
> *wĕtiqwātĕkā lô tikkārēt*
> Do not envy sinners in your thoughts,
> but envy the fear of Jahweh every day;
> Then, surely there will be a future (for you),
> And your hope will not be disappointed.

The above translation differs to some extent from existing translations and forces us therefore to elucidate the main problem-areas. The first problem emerges when dealing with the linguistic structure of the admonition in v. 17.

It is difficult to decide whether in such cases (as v. 17), one has to accept the presence of one or two admonitions. Graphically only one Vetitive (*ʾal-yĕqannēʾ*) occurs, but grammatically and semantically a second imperative is presupposed in v. 17b. It is therefore incorrect to interpret v. 17b as a nominal sentence in which the verb *hyh* is omitted. Accordingly

---

[42] Cf. also Prov 6 25–26 and 29 17 with motivations in the form of result-descriptions (although in 29 17 the motive clause grammatically constitutes an ordinary asyndetic subordinate clause).

the preposition *bĕ* in v. 17b is interpreted in relation with the omitted verb[43]. In fact, we have here a typical form of verb-deletion as a form of reduction. The Imperative form of the verb *qn'* is omitted in v. 17b. The resemblance of the preposition *bĕ* in the prepositional phrase reflects the grammatical coherence of the preposition *bĕ* and the deleted verb *qn'*. To be more exact, we could draw the following deep structure of this sentence to demonstrate the verb-deletion:

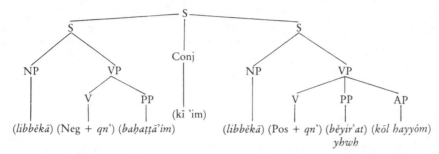

The verb *qn'* clearly functions in both sentences, but in the trans-formation to the surface structure it is deleted by the transformational rule which is called verb-deletion[44].

Considering the context, one must agree with D. Winton Thomas that *yir'at yhwh* in v. 17 is used as the antithesis of *ḥaṭṭā'îm*, but not in the sense that those who fear Jahweh must be envied[45]. Reference is made to the *yir'at yhwh* as the object of *qn'*. In contrast to those who violated the order of Jahweh and missed their destination in life (*ḥaṭṭā'îm*), one must envy the *yir'at Jahweh*, the perfect religious attitude − in order and in harmony with Jahweh's order (that means to be wise: Cf. 1 7 etc.). Then there will be no misfortune and disappointment (cf. the motivation in v. 18).

The motivation, by means of a result-description, sets forth the rewards of piety. Putting one's *qn'* in the *yir'at yhwh*, means identification with the godly rule and order which cannot ever end in illusion or misfortune (as in the case of the sinners). The motivation as a result-description makes clear the worth of putting one's envy in the *yir'at Jahweh*, and by doing that one's hope (expectation of life) is real and not a catastrophical illusion (with regard to the sinners).

It is further quite unnecessary to support the LXX reading of *τηρήσῃς αὐτά* on behalf of the MT[46]. The *kî* introduces the motivation and the attached *'im* must be considered as assertive.

---

[43] Cf. the Afrikaans translation, the translation of R.B.Y. Scott op. cit. 140−141 and the NEB translation.

[44] Cf. Langacker, R. W., Language and its structure, 1968, 121 ff.

[45] Thomas, D. Winton, VT 15 (1965) 274.

[46] Cf. Gemser, B. op. cit. 87; McKane, W. op. cit. 387 and Scott, R.B.Y. op. cit. 141 (which emendates the text according to Prov 24 14).

In v. 17 and v. 18 a perfect example of *homoioteleuton* occurs in the
form:

$$
\left.\begin{array}{l} a-b \\ \\ c-d \end{array}\right] 17
$$

$$
\left.\begin{array}{l} c-d \\ \\ e-d \end{array}\right] 18
$$

The transition of the admonition to the motivation is achieved by the
repetition of *kî ʾim*. It is further noteworthy that the admonition in v. 17
and its motivation in v. 18 form a chiasm:

$$
\begin{array}{c}
17a \searchar 17b \\
18a \nearrow 18b
\end{array}
$$

It is even possible that the author of this saying, which semantically
forms a chiasm, tried to concretise this chiasm poetically by word
symbiosis: cf. *kî ʾim* (twice) and *qnʾ* and *qwh*.

3.1.4 Admonition – Motivation in a Causal Clause

This group of admonitions is probably the most common in usage. It
is even possible that the original form of the admonition consists of one
Imperative (or Vetitive) and is then motivated by means of an attached
causal clause (cf. eg. 24 13a 23 9[47] 26 25 27 1 27 13 and 4 23).

We will only discuss a few instances of this common kind of
admonitions.

Prov 24 1–2

Earlier we referred to this admonition and tried to make it plain why
we classified the motivation in v 2 as a causal clause and not as a result-
description as in v. 20.

Prov 22 22–23

22 *ʾal-tigzol-dāl kî dal-hûʾ*
   wĕʾal-tĕdakkēʾ ʿonî baššāʿar
23 *kî-yhwh yārîb rîbam*
   wĕqābaʿ ʾet-qōbĕʿêhɛm nāpɛš

22 Because a man is poor, do not therefore cheat him,
   nor, at the city gate, oppress anybody in affliction;
23 for Jahweh takes up their cause,
   and extorts the life of their extortioners. (JB)

---

[47] Cf. Onchesheshonqy 7:3–4 and Achiqar A2:62.

The admonition consists of two Vetitive forms and the motivation (v. 23) is attached in the form of a causal clause, introduced by *kî*.

Reference is made in the admonition to the violation of the rights of the poor and especially to the practice of legal proceedings for oppressing the underprivileged[48].

The motivation makes clear that Jahweh acts on behalf of the rights of the underprivileged and might be called their patron[49] (cf. our discussion of Prov 23 10–11).

Prov 3 11–12

11 *mûsar yhwh bĕnî ʾal-timʾās*
    wĕʾal-tāqōṣ bĕtôkaḥtô
12 *kî ʾɛt-ʾăšɛr yɛʾĕhab yhwh yôkîaḥ*
    ûkĕʾāb ʾɛt-bēn yirṣɛh

11 Reject not, my son, the discipline of Jahweh,
    and spurn not his reproof,
12 For those whom Jahweh loves he reproves,
    and that as a father his son whom he loves.

At this point we will restrict ourselves to just a few remarks on this proverb. Its position in the poem (v. 1–12) will be discussed later. The admonition, consisting of two Vetitive forms in a chiastic pattern, warns against the disdain of Jahweh's discipline. The *mûsar* as parallel of *tôkeḥâ*, must be interpreted in the stronger sense of chastisement. In other words, reference is made to the acceptance of suffering.

The motivation, beginning with *kî* and VS, in a causal clause says why suffering must be accepted. The reference to the personal (individual) relation of Jahweh and man be means of the father-son relationship is definitely a variation on the traditional understanding of suffering (cf. Job 5 17–18 and Ps 94 12–13) within the framework of the doctrine of retribution.

Prov 25 21–22

21 *ʾim-rāʿēh śōnaʾăkā haʾăkilēhû lɛḥɛm*
    wĕʾim-ṣāmēʾ hašĕqēhû māyim
22 *kî gɛḥālîm ʾattâ ḥotɛh ʿal-rōʾsô*
    wayhwh yĕšallɛm-lāk

21 If your enemy is hungry, give him food to eat;
    if he is thirsty, give him water to drink;
22 so you will heap glowing coals on his head,
    and Jahweh will reward you.

---

48 Cf. the explanation of the *dkʾ baššāʿar* by R. de Vaux, Ancient Israel, its life and institutions, 1961, 152 ff. Cf. also Ex 23 6 33 1 and compare also Amenemope Chapters 4 and 20 (ANET 422 and 424).
49 Cf. Fensham, F. C., JNES 21 (1962), 129–139, and Uys, P. de V., NGTT 9 (1968), 183–185.

This proverb is quoted by Paul in Rom 12 20, and it would seem as if this fact alone was enough to occasion volumes of comment on it.

The admonition is formulated in a typically casuistic style (cf. also 26 25) — specifying the condition under which the admonition is true. It seems plausible that the casuistic style is used in this admonition which regulates one's behaviour to one's enemy, because a positive behaviour towards the enemy[50] under all circumstances hardly fits within the doctrine of retribution (cf. also Prov 24 17–18).

However, the motivation in v. 22 creates the main problem of interpretation.

Toy gives an explanation generally accepted, although it is not always understood in the same way:

Do good, because it will bring reward[51].

The heaping of live coals on someone's head is probably a metaphor deriving from a rite of reconciliation that once existed in Egypt[52]. The convicted then carried a pan filled with live coals on his head as a sign of his change of mind (of reconciliation). Thus understood, an enemy to whom kindness is shown, should change his enmity and his revenge.

Gemser and McKane consider v. 22b as secondary[53]. Verse 22b, however, suits the stylistic pattern of v. 21–22, and is strengthened by the LXX reading.

The usage of the verb šillēm in v. 22b, must be interpreted within the context of the act-consequence relation of the older wisdom. The deed of kindness shown to an enemy, will be rewarded by God himself. Hence, it is Jahweh who in the end accomplishes the act-consequence-coherence!

Prov 23 1–3

1 *kî-tēšēb lilḥôm 'et-môšēl*
  bîn tābîn 'et-'ăšer lĕpānêkā
2 *wĕśamtā śakkîn bĕlō'ɛkā*
  'im-ba'al nɛpɛš 'attâ
3 *'al-tit'āw lĕmaṭ'ammôtâw*
  wĕhû lɛḥɛm kĕzābîm
1 When you sit down to eat with a ruler,
  confine your attention to what is before you,
2 and put a knife in your throat,
  if you have a hearty appetite.
3 Do not let your appetite be whetted by his tit-bits,
  for it is deceptive food. (McKane op.cit. 246).

---

50 Cf. the following text concerning the enemy: Ex 23 4–5 Deut 22 1–4 I Sam 24 18–20 Prov 20 22 24 17–18 and Achiqar IX, 171.
51 Toy, C. H. op.cit. 468. Cf. also Whybray, R.N., The Book of Proverbs, 1972, 149.
52 Cf. Morenz, S., Feurige Kohlen auf dem Haupt, ThLZ 78 (1953), 187–192. Cf. also von Rad, G. op.cit. 177f.
53 Gemser, B. op.cit. 113 and McKane, W. op.cit. 591–592.

The admonition consists of the entire v 1–3a and is, interestingly enough, variously formulated in three commands. The form *bîn tābîn* must be considered as a whole and is exhortative in character. *bîn* must be taken as an Absolute Inf. The *waw Consecutive* + Perf. in v. 2, parallel to v. 1, should also be interpreted as an Imperative. It is only possible if *bîn tābîn* as a whole is taken as Imperative in meaning. It is not clear, therefore, why Richter described the form in v. 1 as »heischendes Präsens«[54]. The third admonition is in ordinary Vetitive form.

Observe also that the admonition assumes a typically casuistic style. It is probably due to this feature that there is no direct Imperative in v. 1. It is impossible to isolate the three admonitions from the motivation in v. 3b[55].

The admonitions are not mere prescriptions for table manners (cf. the translation of JB), but the crucial point is that you are at the table of the *môšēl* and the food might be *lɛḥɛm kĕzābîm* (deceptive food). But in which sense is this food deceptive? McKane maintains that the food is not offered without genuine hospitality, but the deceptiveness of the food lies in the very fact that »a public exhibition of gluttony by an ambitious official will damage his prospects and may prove to be his undoing[56].« The present author is not convinced whether the deceptive food would be as positive as McKane assumes. Would it not be possible to paraphrase as following: Vindicate your selfrespect and stand by your manners[57] so that you do not infringe the table of the ruler visibly. This would be an instrument to get you in his power. In other words: retain diplomatic objectivity!

Considering the comparable prescription of Amenemope (XXIII, 13–20) one could suggest that the natural respect (order) between ruler and subject is here at issue. But even then the explanation of the »deceptive food« is not clear.

As an introduction of the motivation one would expect the particle *kî*, but in v. 3b the *waw* occurs. Whether asyndetic or not, this *waw* can only be interpreted in a causal clause and is therefore classified as such.

The following admonitions with motivations in causal clauses are not discussed in full, although their peculiarities will be considered in the conclusions at the end: Prov 4 1–2a 4 13 4 23 6 20–23[58] 7 24–27 and 8 10–11.

---

54 Richter, W. op. cit. 38.
55 Erroneously treated by Zeller, D. op. cit. 21–22 and Toy, C. H. op. cit. 428.
56 McKane, W. op. cit. 382. According to Postel, J. op. cit. 101, the deception also referred to that of the guest: »He must carefully consider his own response to the elaborate display at the ruler's table, an obvious indication of position and wealth«.
57 Prescriptions on behaviour are not unusual in the Ancient Near East, cf. Ptaḥ Ḥotep 120 and Amenemope XXIII, 13–20.
58 The admonition and motivation are divided by a benediction (v. 22) which functions as a secondary motivation.

3.1.5   Admonition – Motivation in Predication

Some scholars would entertain reservation in accepting some of the following occurrences within the framework of this heading. In cases where the predication is introduced by *kî*, one could think of an ordinary causal relation. It is not entirely wrong, but the form and content of the sentence(s) attached to the particle *kî* are here considered to be decisive for the purpose of classification.

Prov 14 7

lēk minnɛgɛd lĕʾîš kĕsîl
ûbal-yādaʿtā śiptê-dāʿat
Go from the presence of a foolish man,
for lips of knowledge you have not noticed.

The verb clause in v. 7b of MT and the text-critical proposal to read *ûbal taḥad*[59] are, grammatically speaking, difficult to grasp. The latter is also text-critically difficult to explain.

The reading of the LXX seems more likely in this context. Verse 7b then reads: *ûkĕlî-dāʿat śiptê-dāʿat*. (Translated: for a vessel/garment of knowledge is sensible words (lips)).

The consonantal difference with the MT could be ascribed to reading (b) instead of (k) (orthographically the characters are related). The *yod* is identified with the following character (d) instead of the previous (1).

According to the above, the motivation in v. 7b is a predication of wisdom's ethos on reticence (cf. Prov 10 11 10 19 10 20 10 31–32 11 12 18 2, etc.) and might be compared with Prov 20 15.

The sense of the predication attached to the admonition (v. 7a) as motivation, is to describe the quality of the wise words and the resignation of the wise to blow off a lot of words (nonsense) as a fool. Extra precaution must be taken in the presence of a fool.

Prov 23 31–36

The admonition occurs in v. 31 and is directed against a too strong desire for alcoholic wine (to put it lightly). The predication of drunkenness and the hangover stage functions clearly as a motivation for the admonition. It must be noted further that the admonition in v. 31 is embedded within a predication which already starts in v. 29.

Prov 4 1 and 2b–9

One might consider the admonition in v. 2(b) apart from the admonition in v. 1, but contextually it would be better to maintain the unity

---

[59] Cf. Gemser, B. op. cit. 66. Also followed by McKane, W. op. cit. 464. Cf. also Postel, J. op. cit. 37, for his attempt to declare *bal* as a »poetic synonym« for *lô*.

of v. 1–9[60]. Verse 2(b) is not to be isolated completely from v. 1. The unity is somewhat disrupted by the intersection of the motivation in v. 2a on part of the admonition in v. 1. The admonition in v. 1, which resembles the technical opening of a wisdom teaching, makes it possible to introduce a secondary motivation. It further manifests the almost stereotype collaboration of admonition and motivation.

The motivation in v. 3 ff. takes on the form of a predication of the wisdom teacher's education, which he received from his parents.

Noteworthy is the fact that the predication consists of a further range of admonitions, each followed by a motivative clause.

Reference is made in the motivations to the fact that the teacher acts *in loco parentis*; hence he is an authoritative person in as far as his education is an extension of tradition, but the individual admonitions do not refer for their validity and credibility to the authority of the teacher. The credibility of the admonition must be sought in the content (logic or truth) of the motivation. As long as we do not recognise this coherence of admonition and motivation with regard to its authority, we will lack understanding in the school of the wise.

Prov 4 14–19

The admonition in v. 14–15 contains not less than six Imperatives (Vetitives). They are directed against the wicked and evil men. The motivation in v. 16–19 is a predication of the very nature of the wicked and their destiny in contrast with that of the righteous.

Prov 4 20–22

The exordium of the teacher's lesson is stereotype in style (cf. 4 1 and 4 10), but is intensified through more personal involvement in v. 20–21. The almost staccato style (cf. the changed position of the verb in v. 20 and v. 21) of the admonition increases the need to state why the pupil should listen. The motivation clearly testifies to this importance: these words *are* the life for those who find them[61]!

The introduction of the motivation by *kî* in v. 22 clearly provides a causal relation. But, contextually, emphasis is laid on the predication of the words of the teacher. This predication is crucial in this context, and therefore we consider this motivation a predication which is causally introduced

---

[60] The NEB reversed the order of v. 6 and v. 7. R. N. Whybray op. cit. 30 maintains v. 6–9 as a secondary addition to v. 1–5, because of the use of the feminine form from v. 6 and onwards. The use of the feminine form in v. 6 ff. seems to be quite logical, because in v. 6–9 reference is made to the exceptional value of wisdom, whereas in v. 1–5 reference is made to the instruction of the teacher which he received from his father (tradition).

[61] Compare the difference with 4 4 and 4 10. Like the *tôrâ*, wisdom teaching is the life for him who seeks it!

by *kî*. In the same way the coherence between admonition and motivation in Prov 1 8–9 and 1 15–18 may be described.

Prov 5 1–6

The admonition in two Imperative forms reflects again the traditional invitation or exhortation of listening to wisdom teaching. Whereas in style always the same, it almost every time varies in vocabulary (cf. 1 8 2 1 3 1 3 11 4 1 4 10 4 20, etc.). It is therefore not a coincidence that for the first time we meet the admonition to listen to the *tĕbûnâ* of the wisdom teacher[62]. The admonition in v. 1 is followed by a final clause of purpose in v. 2 and in v. 3–6 the actual motivation follows as a predication of the *zārâ*.

As an aside, observe that the admonition which demands obedience to wisdom teaching is here directly motivated with a predication of the *zārâ*. In view of the almost incredible (but far-reaching) tradition concerning wisdom and the *zārâ*, I wish only to observe here that the predication of the *zārâ* makes it clear that she is the antithesis of wisdom and in fact a substitute for the wicked and evil[63]!

Prov 6 6–8

The admonition (in three Imperatives) in v. 6 is a warning to the sluggard, which is then motivated with a predication (v. 7–8) of the willingness of the ant. The relative particle *'ăšɛr* is enough to demonstrate the coherence of admonition and motivation. The predication can only have the function of a motivation.

Prov 8 5–9

Our interest is mainly concerned in the smaller structural unit, although the global composition cannot be ignored totally[64].

The admonition (v. 5–6aα) which is directed to the *pĕtā'îm* and *kĕsîlîm* is followed by the motivation (introduced by *kî* in v. 6aβ which in this case is a predication of the worth of the teaching of the wisdom. The predication takes the form of a self-recommendation of the wisdom. The predication of wisdom is continued in v. 12ff. after an insection of a similar admonition and its direct motivation (v. 11). It must further be noted that even this motivation is not the final one for it is linked to the final motivation in v. 34–36. The whole poem is built up by the repetition of the admonition and the increased importance of the motivation.

---

[62] We cannot deal here with all these words occurring in the invitation of the wisdom teaching.

[63] Cf. also Chapter 7 and compare Chapter 4 on the wicked and the evil.

[64] Cf. Kayatz, C. op. cit. 74ff. and Skehan, P. W., CBQ 41 (1979), 365–379, for discussions on the structure of Chapter 8.

Prov 23 26–28

The admonition (v. 26) reflects the typical life-setting of the school in appealling to the pupils for attention.

The motivation (v. 27–28) as a predication of a prostitute, following directly on the admonition, points to a certain extent in the direction of what we already discussed in 5 1–6. The question arises: What is the logical link between admonition and motivation? The logical basis of this coherences lies in the preference of the author for words with an ambiguity in usage. »Give your heart« and »have pleasure« put forward the logical tie. Instead of an extension of the admonition with »do not give your hart to« and »do not have pleasure« in a prostitute (whore), the original admonition is directly followed by the predication of the whore.

Prov 23 6–8

The motivation (v. 7–8), follows on the admonition in v. 6. The motivation takes the form of a predication of the *ra˘ ˓āyin* and his so-called hospitality, which is only a means to reach his goal. The one who accepts it, injures himself. Verse 8 cannot be excluded from v. 7. It is in fact an elaboration of the motivation in v. 7.

Prov 23 4–5

The admonition (v. 4) warns against a lust after wealth. The motivation that follows in v. 5[65] takes the form of a simile. This form of predication makes clear (in this text) that wealth is totally undependable. The man who knows his position in this world and knows that this world order is created by Jahweh, realizes the triviality and futility of wearing oneself out in an effort to get rich for the sake of being rich. This attitude might bring total misfortune, because it is no goal in itself and as such even more unattainable than an eagle in the sky[66]. One canot just grasp it if one thinks he is in the position to do so.

Prov 2/ 23–24

Just one text-critical emendation is required here: read *˒ôṣar* (cf. BH.) instead of *nēzɛr*. Verse 24b is then translated: . . . »nor is wealth for generations.« Although the motivation in v. 24[67] apparently consists of two aphorisms, it is classified as a predication. The aphorism intend a description of the reality of wealth (an property) and its relation to personal responsibility and involvement.

---

[65] There is no reason to accept v. 5a as a gloss or an emendation of the verse, cf. Toy, C. H. op. cit. 429. The use of the verb ˓*wp* with eyes as subject forms an integral part of the simile.

[66] Cf. Delitzsch, F. op. cit. 103–108.

[67] Verse 24 is, strictly speaking, not to be excluded from the rest of the sayings (v. 25–27).

The meaning of this admonition and motivation is not just a commendation of a farming career[68], nor is it a polemic against the abundance of the traders: it does not promote agriculture as the ideal profession[69]. Rather, responsibility for property and its use, for economical order, is stressed. This order is as essential as is the order of seasons.

Prov 5 18b–20

The sructure of the poem in Chapter 5 will be discussed later. Verse 18b forms a new admonition: take pleasure in the wife of your youth. The motivation in v. 19 is a predication of the first wife. The predication clearly takes the form of a metaphor and tends towards the lyric style of the Song of Songs.

The rhetorical question in v. 20 definitely forms part of the motivation, because v. 19b and c forms a chiastic pattern with 20: abbc/a. Semantically v. 18b–20 can be excluded from the rest of Chapter 5.

Prov 22 28

'al tassēg gĕbûl 'ôlām
'ăšer 'āśû 'ăbôtêkā
Do not remove the ancient boundary stones,
those which your ancestors established.

Apparently there follows no motivation[70] on the admonition in v. 28a. But the attribute 'ôlām and the predication of the boundary stones in the relative clause (v. 28b) immediately advances the idea that these boundary stones are established (fixed) by the forefathers. It is a part of the heritage and as such, irreplaceable. The act in question not only tramples upon the rights of the fellow man or widow (cf. discussion on Prov 23 10 and also Prov 15 25), but also violates the order of Jahweh who gives each his land (cf. Deut 19 14) and sees to it that these rights are respected. No wonder the motivation in Prov 23 11 mentions the fact of Jahweh's guardianship of landorder.

The characterization of the boundary stones as 'ôlām and the reference to the 'ābôtēkâ indicate that the property is inalienable and inviolable[71].

Prov 27 10

rē'ăkā wĕrē'ah (MT) 'ăbîkā 'al-ta'ăzōb
ûbêt 'āḥîkā 'al-tābô' bĕyôm 'êdɛkâ
ṭôb šākēn qārôb mē'aḥ rāḥôq

---

[68] Postel, J. op. cit. 81.
[69] Ringgren, H., Sprüche/Prediger, 1962, 108.
[70] Postel, J. op.cit. 107 denies a motivation in this case. We must however, take the context into consideration in determining whether there is a motivation or not. The introductory particles like kî lĕma'an, etc. do not always occur.
[71] Cf. McKane, W. op. cit. 379.

Do not neglect your own friend or your fathers's
And to the house of your brother go not in the day of your calamity:
A neighbour at hand is better than a brother far away.

Gemser and Scott[72] suggested the deletion of v. 10b (cf. BH) in order to establish a better coherence between v. 10a and v. 10c. McKane stated that there is no intrinsic connection between v. 10a and v. 10c. To make it even more complicated, Toy noted a discrepancy between v. 10b and Prov 17 17. Even if solved, v. 10c must be considered as an independent aphorism[73].

The coherence between v. 10a and v. 10b must be taken as in the MT. The emendation of *tabûz* for *tābô'* and *dayyɛkkā* (cf. BH) would not simplify the coherence of v. 10b and 10c and would in fact impute the bad behaviours to the subject of v. 10b and not to the brother. Such an interpretation would surely disturb the ethics of v. 10.

Verse 10a and v. 10b are two admonitions. The coherence of 10a and 10b must be seen as follows: v. 10a is strengthened by v. 10b, and states the importance of the family friend in situations where one's brother might derive benefit from one's trouble. It clearly reflects a covetous attitude of the brother. In this sense v. 10b increases the importance of the father's friend, and also states the circumstances in which it is of crucial importance. When this point of view is accepted, there is no conflict between v. 10b and Prov 17 17. Both sayings are true in their own right.

Verse 10c is not an *independent* aphorism. The coherence of v. 10c with the preceding might be described as asyndetic, but it is unquestionably to be taken as a motivative clause. The motivative clause is without an introductory particle which might be explained from the usage of a popular proverb as motivation. Verse 10c is most likely an ordinary popular proverb which is here used to predicate the friend who ties in with your need and is at your disposal in times of trouble, without being cunningly alert for possible profit that he could gain from your trouble. The 'āḥ rāḥôq is the brother who must be avoided in such times of trouble, but the real friend in need is the proverbial friend indeed.

Another problematic proverb occurs in Collection D:

Prov 24 29
'al-tō'mar ka'ašɛr 'āśāh-lî kēn 'ɛ'ɛ́śɛh-lô
'āšîb lā'îš kĕpo'ōlô
Say not: I will do to him as he did to me,
I will repay the man for his deed.

At first sight one might question the function of v. 29 as a real admonition, because it is clearly linked with the preceding and has in fact as

---

[72] Gemser, B. op. cit. 96—97 and Scott, R.B.Y. op. cit. 161.
[73] Toy, C. H. op. cit. 485—486.

such a motivative function. This, however, does not deny the fact that v. 29 still functions as a secondary admonition. Then again it might seem as if no motivation is attached to the admonition in v. 19a. Instead of a direct motivative clause, a quotation of the prohibited words occurs. The statement claims the exceptional prerogative of God or the king as judge (cf. Prov 20 22). The determination of what must be repaid is in the hands of the judge. One dare not think he is the judge in a case against his neighbour, possibly nursing a spirit of revenge within himself. Do not bluff yourself thinking you only exact proper repayment for what he owes you!

The quotation in v. 19b is therefore acceptable as a motivation (for v. 19a), which we can classify as a factual-description (*Sachverhaltbeschreibung*).

3.1.6   Admonition — Motivation as a Promise

An interesting group of admonitions is that whose motivations are promises. One may ask why these admonitions are motivated with promises. Why is wisdom-counsel motivated with such theologically pregnant motivations? Several reasons might be offered, but let us proceed to the various admonitions themselves.

Prov 1 23

Linguistically the proverb can be divided into an admonition (v. 23a) and a motivation (v. 23b and c)[74].

The personified wisdom acts as a prophet in v. 20 ff. It is almost a call to repentance. The salvation results from acceptance of wisdom's discipline!

Wisdom as the prophetic word makes it possible to find a motivation in the form of a promise (cf. Joel 2 28).

Prov 3 1-2

The admonition (v. 1) is the demand of the wisdom, as priestly *tôrâ*, of obedience to commandments.

Although the motivative clause is introduced by *kî*, it nevertheless introduces a promise. This kind of promise is typical of the Deuteronomistic Law (cf. Deut 6 2 8 1 4 40 Ex 20 12, etc.)[75].

The wisdom-counsel is called *tôrâ* and motivated with a promise so typical in Coll. A. Thus, definite traces can be found here of an identification of wisdom-counsel with *tôrâ*-stipulation, which represents a typical phenomenon in the development of tradition in Prov 1—9.

Prov 3 5-6

The admonition is relatively long (v. 5-6a) and the motivation functions as a short promise (introduced with *waw*).

---

[74] Cf. the discussion of Prov 1 20-23 under »Complex Structures«.

[75] Cf. also the promise in Prov 4 4 4 10 and 7 2.

In contrast with Prov 1 20 ff. wisdom represents itself as the priestly *tôrâ* in this chapter (cf. v. 1 in comparison with Deut 8 1 and 30 16). The individual is demanded to trust wholeheartedly in Jahweh, to have no faith in his own perception, but to *know* (the increased parallel to *trust*) Jahweh in every circumstance of life. The attached final clause is undoubtedly a promise in function. The motivation emphasizes the trust in Jahweh's sovereignty. He himself is the one who guides life to its fulfilment.

Prov 3 9–10

In a very similar fashion (as the preceding) the motivation (v. 10) undoubtedly functions as a promise.

Presumably we find cultic instructions in this chapter in which the wisdom acts as the priest. The cultic instructions make us aware of the sacrifices and tell us that the best of one's property and income belongs to God. By this admonition one is warned not to fall victim of one's own avarice and to consider that possession is but a gift of Jahweh (cf. Deut 26 1ff.). That explains why v. 9 is motivated with a promise so typical in D (Deut 28 8) and in the Prophets (cf. Mal 3 10–12). Those who relate their possession to Jahweh, will benefit from his abundance.

Prov 3 21–26

The direct admonition occurs in v. 21 and the motivation in the form of a promise in v. 22 ff. But, if we take the context of the entire Chapter 3 into consideration, we find that v. 19 (referring to the cosmic role of wisdom and the role of wisdom in God's acts of creation) introduces the main motivation for the whole chapter. Wisdom is the law of nature and real (orderly) existence means a life consciously devoted to wisdom. Within this context the admonition (v. 21) and the motivation (v. 22 ff.) as promise make sense. The motivation makes clear that those people who live an orderly life in compliance with wisdom will obtain real life — in harmony with the cosmic order, without sudden disaster and destruction (cf. v. 25).

One might assume v. 25–26 to be a separate admonition with a motivative clause. It is, however, impossible to isolate v. 25 contextually from the rest of the motivation (v. 22–26) and therefore we maintain it as a motivation in admonition form. Graphically we may illustrate the coherence as follows:

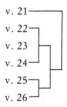

Prov 3 7–8

This admonition explicates the ethics of modesty (cf. Is 5 21 10 20 Jer 9 22). What is the prescription of wisdom in obtaining a moderate estimation of one's merits? Self-esteem precludes wisdom. For obtaining real wisdom two principles must be recognised: the *yĕrā' 'et-Jahweh* and *sûr mērā'*[76]. The contents of both these principles will be discussed later.

The motivation, without any introductory particles, is here best taken as a promise, although it leaves open the possibility of a »wish«. The frequent use of the promise as motivation would support the same use in v. 8. But why is v. 7 motivated with the promise (wish) of physical healing? One might reason that according to the wisdom a direct coherence exists between evil and physical sickness. But, whether this is meant in this context is controversial. It could possibly be that v. 8 is the explication of a particular example in which the effects of evil are demonstrable. Evil affects every bit of orderly existence, and in this sense bodily destruction and sickness is not totally excluded from the individual involvement in the act of evil (sin), or let us say, in compliance with sin.

Although the following proverbs are of importance for our theological interpretation in the end it is not necessary to discuss their linguistic structure in full: cf. Prov 4 4 4 5–6a 4 6b and 4 7–9. The motivation, (as a promise) in each occurrence is introduced by the *waw*.

Notable is the fact that the promise, as motivation, only occurs in Collection A (Prov 1–9). It appears as if it is a tendency in the younger wisdom, most probably influenced by the Deuteronomist and the prophets. The admonitions, which are motivated by promises, always refer to wisdom-related behaviour (mainly the personified wisdom) and Jahweh. Only two admonitions (3 5–6 and 3 9–10), draw the attention to the correct religious attitude towards Jahweh, which is intelligible within the context of Chapter 3, in which wisdom acts as the cultic priest. The other admonitions are concerned with the acquisition of wisdom and the keeping of the principles of wisdom. The connecting motivations make it clear that wisdom is not mere wisdom counsel, but of an importance equal to that of the Deuteronomistic law. Wisdom becomes in fact the *dĕbar Jahweh* – the prophetic word. Thus, it clarifies the promise of life[77], extension of life and the qualitative fulfilment of existence in compliance with wisdom.

3.1.7   Admonition – Motivation in an Interrogative Clause

Although we maintain a separate sub-division for those admonitions with motivations in interrogative clauses (which give recognition to a differ-

---

[76] It is the first time that these two main principles occur in the same saying, which is theologically of crucial importance.

[77] Cf. Schmitt, E., Leben in den Weisheitsbüchern Job, Sprüche und Jesus Sirach, 1954, 76 ff. and 139 ff.

ent grammatical formulation), there will be no separate category in our index of reference. The interrogative particle is not enough reason for a distinctive classification.

Prov 24 28

Verse 28b is undoubtedly a motivative clause, even if we accept an imperative translation (cf. Gemser 90) instead of an interrogative translation. The coherence between admonition and motivation can be described as a causal relation. The motivation (in rhetorical form) makes clear that false witness[78] against a neighbour is objectionable. In committing perjury, one is playing into the hands of the evil, for the legal-process is to reflect the order of Jahweh through which the truth is revealed. A wicked and false judge or witness must therefore be condemned in harsh words.

Prov 22 26–27

Only one admonition is mentioned explicitly in v. 26(a), although in parallel admonitions in v. 22 and v. 24 two imperative (Vetitive) forms occur. It seems evident that verb-deletion (cf. 23 17–18 24 14 and 8 10) was an important syntactical device in the *Parallelismus membrorum* to create a sound rhythm[79].

The motivation (v. 27), although containing the interrogative particle *lāmmâ*[80], embraces a result-description: People who easily give guarantees or pledge themselves as surety for other people, run the risk of loosing their property and might suffer from their ill deeds[81].

Prov 5 15–18a

The admonition in v. 15 which demands sexual satisfaction with one's own wife, is directly attached to the preceding description of the »strange« woman (cf. our discussion on the complex structures). The motivation in v. 16[82]. starts with a metaphoric wisdom-saying (Aussage) one would assume, but seeing that it is followed by a direct answer in v. 17, one should rather maintain v. 16 as a rhetorical question. Verse 18a then follows as a wish which is immediately followed by another admonition (v. 18b).

---

[78] In the wisdom literature physical organs of speech are often used when referring to the speech itself; cf. Bühlmann, W., Vom rechten Reden und Schweigen, 1976, 13f.

[79] Future research might prove that, in occurrences of Verb-deletion as a means of constructing rhythm, the word-rhythm in Hebrew poetry must not be over-estimated on behalf of an accent-rhythm.

[80] Cf. also the motivation in Prov 5 19b on the admonition in Prov 5 18b–20.

[81] In Ancient Israel it was forbidden to charge interest on a loan (Ex 22 25). With foreigners it was different (cf. Deut 15 3 Ex 22 26–27 and Deut 24 10–13). Cf. de Vaux, R. op. cit. 170–172.

[82] There is not enough reason to emendate v. 16a to be a final clause with *pɛn* or a secondary demand with a Vetitive.

The motivation warns against a too generous (!) attitude towards other women which might result in a similar attitude of the wife who goes out on the street and be generous to other men: the fatal circle. The connected wish-clause shows clearly the high premium placed on the monogamous marriage.

The classification of this motivation still requires attention. This metaphorical saying (with its explication) concerning the real wife would best be classified as a predication.

3.1.8   Admonition − Motivation in a Conditional Clause

There is only one example of such motivations, Prov 24 27:

hākēn bahûṣ mĕla'kĕtɛkā
wĕ'attĕdāh baśśādê lāk
'aḥar ûbānîtā bêtɛkā
Set in order your work out of doors,
Make it ready on the land;
Then establish yourself a house (family).

The admonition consists of two imperative forms, but the motivation in v. 27c is without any introductory particles like *kî, pɛn, lĕma'an*, etc. In fact, one finds here a temporal conditions clause: you can build a house (start a family[83]) only if you take the correct precautions. The correct sequence of operation is indicated. One must get things in order before you start to work towards your goal. The other way round means failure and misfortune.

The majority of scholars[84] maintain that this proverb is isolated from both the preceding and the following verses. The argumentation is, however, inconclusive. The appearance of an isolated saying within the context of Collection D, 24 23−24, in which certain topics form a regular sequence, is inconceivable.

It is most likely that v. 27 was a popular proverb with its own proper meaning, which has become metaphorically attached to v. 24 ff. Verse 24 ff. deals with the procedure of the judge, emphasizing the righteousness (justice) of his sentence[85]. In v. 28 f. the interest switches to the perjured witness. According to our understanding v. 27 forms the logical sequence of v. 24−26. The judge must follow the right legal procedure of hearing and testing the witnesses before he sentences somebody. Only then is he capable of judging honestly and maintaining the right order − as referred to in the popular proverb (v. 27).

---

[83]   Cf. Toy, C.H. op. cit. 454.
[84]   Cf. e.g. McKane, W. op. cit. 575−576 and Gemser, B. op. cit. 90.
[85]   Cf. Boecker, H. J., Redeformen des Rechtslebens im Alten Testament, 1964, 123 ff.

3.1.9   Admonition − Motivation in a Secondary Command

In the admonition now to be discussed, the motivation is concealed in a secondary command. Again we pay special attention to this group of motivations in our discussion, but it is not necessary to insert a new category in our index of reference.

Prov 20 13b
pĕqaḥ ʿênêkā
śĕbaʿ lāḥɛm
Keep your eyes open
and you will have enough food.

Although the discussion of v. 13b stands distinct from v. 13a, it does not mean that the two stichoi v. 13 exist without coherence. Indeed, they are closely related.

If we compare v. 13b with v. 13a, it apparently looks as if v. 13b is without a motivative clause, for another demand (*śĕbaʿ*) occurs in v. 13bβ. The function of this secondary Imperative is the same as the final clause in v. 13aβ. Otherwise v. 13bβ would have no sense. To love sleep is to be lazy (v. 13a), but »open your eyes« (stop being lazy) then you will have enough to eat[86]. Thus, in function v. 13bβ is a motivation in a final clause (similar to v. 13aβ)[87].

Prov 13 20a
hōlē(w)k ʾɛt-ḥăkāmîm wɛḥkām (MT)
Walk with the wise and you will become wise.

Attention is given to this proverb, for according to MT it is an admonition with a motivative clause in a secondary Imperative. The function of the motivation might then be to describe the result of the preceding demand.

Text-critically, however, it may be doubted whether we have a real admonition in v. 20a. Verse 20b is formulated in the typical participial form of the wisdom saying (Aussage). Verse 20a, as the antithetic parallel of v. 20b would be sounder with a participle reading (*hōlēk*)[88]. The Imperative form of v. 20a (MT) is probably the result of an interchanging of the consonants *l* and *w* of *hōlēk* (*scriptio plena*). The vocalization of *ḥkm* (v. 20aβ) is adjusted according to the reading of *hlk* by the Masoretes.

Contextually it would therefore be better to maintain v. 20a in the participle form in an ordinary antithetic wisdom saying (Aussage). Verse 20

---

[86] Cf. Lampartner, H., Das Buch der Weisheit, 1975³, 267−268.
[87] Gemser, B. op. cit. 79 and Toy, C. H. op. cit. 388 maintain it as a result clause. It is not only a »abhängige Rede« as W. Richter maintains op. cit. 41.
[88] Cf. the LXX and the Vulgate. Cf. also Zimmerli, W., ZAW 51 (1933), 183.

then reads: He who walks with the wise, will become wise,
But he who associates with fools suffers from it.

Prov 20 22

'al-tō'mar 'ăšallĕmâ-ra'
qawwēh layhwh wĕyōša' lāk[89]
Say not, I shall repay evil for evil
wait for Jahweh to deliver you.

This proverb is one semantic unit. Verse 22b is not a continuation of the admonition in v. 22a, but already begins the motivation for v. 22a. One might think that v. 22b is a distinctive admonition with its own motivation in *wĕyōša' lāk*. This final clause, however, is no general statement about Jahweh's aid for those who wait on him, but the entire v. 22b gives reason not to avenge evil in one's own strength. The focus is on the character of evil and in this respect reference is made to the doctrine of retribution[90].

The relation of admonition (v. 22a) and motivation (v. 22b) may be described as a causal relation.

Prov 3 3–4

The admonition (v. 3) consists of three parallel demands concerning the *ḥɛsɛd wɛ'ĕmɛt* (hendiadys). Verse 4 is another admonition in formulation, but contextually it is a promise in an imperative form.

The acceptance and constant desire for *ḥɛsɛd* and *'ĕmɛt* is motivated by the promise of recognition by Jahweh and the people[91].

Prov 7 2a

šĕmōr miḥwôtay wɛḥyēh
Keep my commandments and live!

Immediately following the general introduction of the wisdom instruction (7 1) is the particular demand, which is motivated by a promise. The grammatical form of the promise is not the ordinary Imperfect, but an Imperative. Whether this Imperative form of the motivation was a special feature of instructive speech is difficult to determine.

Two more examples of motivations in the Imperative occur: Prov 8 33 and 9 5–6. In both cases the motivations are promissory in character.

3.1.10 Admonitions in which the Motivation Precedes the Imperative Form

---

[89] Cf. Prov 25 21–22 and Deut 32 35.
[90] Cf. Scott, R. B. Y. op. cit. 122 and Whybray, R. N. op. cit. 116.
[91] Cf. our discussion on the ethos of the admonitions later.

Before we proceed to some exceptional peculiarities of the admonition form as such, let us examine more closely those admonitions in which the motivation occurs at the beginning. Again it is not necessary to introduce a new category in our index of reference.

Prov 20 19

gôlɛh-sôd hôlēk rākîl
ûlĕpôtê šĕpātâw lô tit'ārāb (cf. Prov 11 13)
The bearer of gossip lets out secrets,
have nothing to do with chatterers.   (JB)

The subject of v. 19a is not the *gôlɛh-sôd* (Gemser op. cit 78 and Bühlmann op cit 238), but it is those who accompany the *rākîl* who let out secrets. The translation of Richter[92] shows a misunderstanding of the structure of v. 19a and its coherence with 19b. The two stichoi form a synthetic parallelism. The *pôtɛh šĕpātâw* directly refers to the *hôlēk râkîl*. The coherence between v. 19a and 19b is that of a normal admonition followed by a motivation. The only difference is the appearance of the motivation (v. 19a) as a wisdom saying before the admonition. The admonition prohibits company with the chatterer. It is motivated by a wisdom saying (Aussage) which gives a predication of the people who associate themselves with the *rākîl*.

It is interesting that *rākîl* is used instead of *kĕsîl*, for, apart from the occurrence above, *rākîl* only occurs in Prov 11 13. It is probably used to give more prominence to the gossiper (who is in fact, a *kĕsîl*), whereas *kesîl* might be too neutral in this respect.

It must be noted further that the Prohibitive form occurs instead of the regular Vetitive form with *'al*. That does not make the admonition irregular and hence it would be textual descrimination to extoll the Prohibitive at the expense of the Vetitive form (on the basis of this text).

More or less the same structure appears in Prov 20 18. If one reads the admonition in v. 18b first, the coherence with the motivation (v. 18a) becomes evident. The coherence is again that of a predication in a regular wisdom saying. The wisdom saying, with its appeal to observation, as predication clarifies the validity of the admonition. War must be conducted with effective strategy and consultation. It is then motivated by the observation that successful plans (operations) are achieved by consultation.

An identical structure is to be found in Prov 17 14 (cf. also 28 17). The admonition occurs at the end of a predication (as motivation) of the very

---

[92] Richter, W. op. cit. 80 and 152: Wer Geheimnisse offenbart, als Verleumder umhergeht, wer einfältig handelt mit seinen Lippen — habe ja keine Gesellschaft (mit ihnen). Cf. also Bühlmann, W. op. cit. 239.

nature of a quarrel. In Prov 31 31 an admonition occurs at the end of a long
predication (as motivation) of the real wife and her virtues[93].

A little more complex is the structure and coherence of the admonition
in

Prov 19 18b

yassēr binĕkā kî-yēš tiqwâ
wĕʾel-hămîtô ʾal-tiśśāʾ napšɛkā
Chastise your son while there is hope,
but be careful not to flog him to death.

A most interesting inter-dependence exists between v. 18a and 18b. The
admonition in v. 18a[94] is evident without v. 18b, but the admonition in
v. 18b cannot stand on its own. This inter-dependence is expressed in the
NEB translation: . . . »but be careful not to flog him to death.«

At first sight it might appear as if v. 18b is only an extension or
repetition of the admonition in v. 18a, but it is also possible that v. 18a
contains the motivation for v. 18b. The killing of the son (pupil) would end
all hope of success whatsoever. Doing so would be the result of bad temper
and immature instruction which leads to such things (v. 19?).

Emphasis is laid on the character of the *mûsār* of the father (teacher)
and on the attitude in which it must be practised. When practised in the
proper way, there is hope for father and son, but when the attitude is
inspired by evil thoughts (v. 18b is most likely to be negative in sense), all
hope is cancelled and the institution of the *mûsār* is violated in every
respect.

In this sense v. 19a is not only an independent admonition, but functions
in a way as motivation of v. 19b.

Another possibility exists for explaining the dependence of v. 18a on
18b: Verse 18b is an explication of *tqwh* (18a). The accent is laid on the *hope*,
connected with the *mûsār* (*ysr*). Because of this hope the father, in
exercising his *mûsār*-task, needs not to think his son so useless (without
hope) that nothing can be done. Because there *is hope* when the *mûsār*[95] is
practised, the father must not think of harming (killing) his child.

3.1.11   An Implicit Admonition − Motivation

An implicit demand might be accepted in some occurrences in
Proverbs, introduced by *ʾim*.

In a couple of occurrences (Prov 24 17−18 25 21−22 1 10−19 6 1−5 and
24 14 (?)) the imperative demand is preceded by a condition (introduced by

---

[93] It would be fascinating to compare the attributes of this »woman« and that of wisdom in
Prov 1−9 and the possibility of her function in contrast with the *zārâ* (Prov 1−9).

[94] Cf. our discussion under 3.1.3.

[95] *ysr* must not be seen exclusively as physical punishment here. Cf. also Postel, J. op. cit. 42.

'*im*) which limits the appropriateness of the admonition. In each protasis, however, an imperative demand occurs. In those cases, introduced by '*im*, without any explicit demand, these might be implicit admonitions: In other words, the admonition is formulated in a casuistic style. The occurrence of the motivation supports such a view.

Prov 2 1–22 is chosen to illustrate the above assumption.

Instead of an imperative form of *šm'* and *lqh*, a casuistic formulation is carried through in v. 1. Apparently the intention of this style is the same as that of the admonition. The occurrence of the motivation (cf. v. 2f.) is therefore not unexpected.

The admonition (?) in the protasis (v. 1) is followed by an explication of the basic demand (compare the embedded final clause in v. 2). The apodosis (introduced by '*āz*) follows in v. 5ff. Extraordinary is the disruption of the apodosis by a secondary motivation (v. 6–8). In v. 9 the apodosis continues and is immediately followed by a motivation (v. 10–11). Three final clauses then follow (cf. v. 12–15 (purpose), v. 16–17 (purpose) and v. 20 (final consequence)). The second and the third final clauses are motivated (cf. v. 18–19 and v. 21–22 respectively). The motivation, v. 21–22, in promissory style (typically Deuteronomistic) is the climax of the whole poem.

Structurally the poem is built up as follows:

Protasis	4v.	v. 1 / v. 2 / v. 3 / v. 4
Apodosis with Jahwistic motivation	4v.	v. 5 / v. 6 / v. 7 / v. 8
Continuation of apodosis with motivation	3v.	v. 9 / v. 10 / v. 11
First final clause (purpose)	4v.	v. 12 / v. 13 / v. 14 / v. 15
Second final clause (purpose) with motivation	4v.	v. 16 / v. 17 / v. 18 / v. 19
The third and main final clause (final consequence) with main motivation	3v.	v. 20 / v. 21 / v. 22

The apodosis is interrupted twice by motivations and parallelling this structure, it is found that the last two final clauses are also interrupted by two motivations. The last motivation, v. 21–22, might also be taken as the main motivation for the admonition (?) in v. 1ff. In this way the circle of reasoning is closed and in the end one could hardly deny the admonitory character of the casuistic introduction.

Prov 24 14 is another difficult example of an implicit admonition:

kēn dēʿê ḥokmâ lĕnapšekā
ʾim-māṣāʾtā wĕyēš ʾaḥărît
wĕtiqwātĕkā lōʾtikkārēt
Such is knowledge of wisdom for your soul:
find it, and there will be a morrow,
and your hope will not be in vain. (JB)

Although the MT maintains an imperative of *ydʿ*, a number of questions arise. Contextually v. 13–14 is one unit. The imperative form of *ydʿ* preceded by *kēn*, with *ḥokmâ* as the direct object is quite unfamiliar.

Gemser[96] suggests the reading of *mĕtûqâ lĕlibbɛkā wĕ* . . . after *dēʿâ* and *ṭōbâ* after *ḥokmâ*. This emendation, based on metri causa, reconstructs the 3 + 3 rhythm. Semantically this emendation represents a correct contextual interpretation[97].

It might be, however, that only one stichos is present in v. 14a. The best proposal then would be: *kēn dēʿâ wĕhokmâ lĕnapšɛkā*. The *kēn* definitely refers to the context of v. 13b (compare the use of honey in connection with wisdom in Prov 16 24). The structure, however, still requires our attention. In v. 13a an admonition occurs (eat honey) together with its motivation (v. 13b): as food and medicament honey is good for one's health. But that is not the main intention of the saying. Verse 13 is only metaphorically applied to wisdom – the best medicine for existence and a good future. The acceptance of wisdom is pure delight. Instead of repeating an imperative which correlates with take (eat honey) in v. 13a, the wholesome character of honey and wisdom is compared: Otherwise the *kēn* in v. 14 is not understandable. Grammatically we might call it sentence-deletion which generates a structural comparison in which the coherence of v. 13 and v. 14 is illuminated. We, therefore, have to maintain an implicit admonition in v. 14a which is not literally expressed because of sentence-deletion.

The conditional introduction, *ʾim*, in v. 14b is also admonitory in character, but is not an independent admonition. It is part of the motivation of wisdom's validity: obedience to wisdom ensures one's future and one's hope will not be in vain.

---

[96] Gemser, B. op. cit. 89.
[97] Etymological suggestions do not satisfy; cf. Thomas, D. W., JTS 38 (1937), 401.

An implicit admonition is probably present in the beatitude (Seligpreisung). The 'ašrê-form obviously has an exhortative function[98]. Classification of this form as an admonition does, however, raise problems. Hence we prefer to see it as an implicit admonition. It has already been observed that the 'ašrê might also occur as part of the motivation (cf. e.g. Prov 8 32). In occurrences such as Prov 3 13 14 21 16 20 28 14 29 18 and 8 34 the intention of the 'ašrê is the same as that of the admonition. It is, therefore, not strange to find connected motivative clauses with these 'ašrê-forms – even if formulated in antithetic parallelisms[99].

3.1.12 Complex Structures

It is plain from the discussion on the structure of Chapter 2 of Proverbs (par. 3.1.11) that the admonition often occurs within larger poems or semantic units. This makes our method of classification difficult, because an exact isolation of the admonition and its motivation is impossible. Structurally it might be possible, but semantically the inter-dependence of sentences often make it impossible to describe the proper function of the motivation. Without entering into a detailed description of the following complex structures, we should look at the following structures:

Prov 23 22–25

According to the MT the admonition in v. 22–23 (Impt-Vetitive and Impt-Vetitive) is followed by a motivation (v. 24–25) in the form of a predication. Text-critically we have a problem with the position and inter-pretation of v. 23. In the LXX version v. 23 is lacking. Gemser and McKane[100] are therfore inclined to maintain v. 23 as secondary.

Verse 24 is clearly linked with v. 22. It would therefore be better to maintain MT, but to invert v. 22 and v. 23. Then we have the general appeal to acquire wisdom and knowledge (compare v. 12 and v. 19 of Chapter 23), following the concrete, particular admonition and then the motivation. The proverb then intends: Buy the best commodities (wisdom and knowledge) on the market. Then follows the particularisation of the general demand: Be obedient to your parents! The motivation combines the general and particular demand with the predication of the parents' joy and blessedness with a wise child.

Prov 22 17–19

The only problem concerning the introduction of Coll. C is the classification of the motivation following on the introductory demand.

---

[98] Cf. Kayatz, K. op.cit. 51 and Wolff, W., Amos' geistige Heimat, 1964, 16–17.

[99] Compare the predication as motivation in Prov 3 14–20 of the 'asrê-form in v. 13. 'ašrê is used instead of the Impt. of mṣ' or pwq.

[100] McKane, W. op.cit. 389.

Although v. 18 is introduced with *kî* which might be interpreted as a causal relation, the intention of v. 18 is a predication of wisdom's worth. We therefore maintain the motivation as a predication. The final clause in v. 19 states the eventual purpose of the admonition and serves also as part of the motivation.

The following discussion on thematic wisdom teachings in Prov 1—9 intends only to illuminate the larger structures, whereas we have till now isolated the individual admonitions.

Prov 1 10–19

Verse 10 warns against seduction by sinners. Verses 11—14 forms not a direct motivation, but a description of the seductiveness of the sinners. With increased intention the admonition (cf. v. 10) is repeated in v. 15. The direct motivation now follows in v. 16—18 in the form of a predication of the final purpose of the evil and its eventual consequences. This motivation is artistically built up around a popular proverb (Sprichwort) in v. 17. Verse 19 concludes with a general judgement in combination with the motivation, but also in reference to the description of the sinners' seduction (v. 11—14).

Structurally this coherenced can be illustrated as follows:

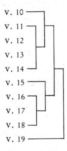

Within this composition it is therefore impossible to isolate the admonition (v. 15) and the motivation (v. 16 f.) entirely from the rest of the poem. Verse 10, which is described by J. Schmidt[101] as the most basic form of the *mashal* and not necessarily semantically dependent on what follows it, is as an admonition, not an independent demand. It cannot be isolated from the motivation and is, therefore, repeated in v. 15 to form a climax.

Prov 1 20–33

This passage contains the »prophetic« invitation and exhortation of personified wisdom. Verse 23 is clearly an admonition, directly followed by a motivation in a promissory form, introduced by *hinnê* and the Cohortative.

The admonition (v. 23) is directed to certain people (*pĕtāyîm* and *lēṣîm*) mentioned in v. 22. In v. 24—31 follows the negative »history« of the

---

[101] Schmidt, J. op. cit. 13.

addressed people and wisdom. Then follows the real motivation in v. 32–33, introduced by *kî*, for the admonition in v. 23. The motivation makes plain why the *pĕtāyîm* and *lēṣîm* are compelled to listen to wisdom, because their errors and complacency lead to destruction. The coherence of the verse can be illustrated as follows:

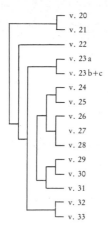

Prov 3 1–12

The passage under discussion reveals a highly poetic structure. This poem is deliberately structured and without the recognition of this structure any attempted interpretation is in jeopardy. We do not claim to highlight all the aesthetic qualities of this poem, and will concentrate only on the sequence of admonition-motivation and its structural unity (whereas our classification only isolated the different admonitions).

Verse 1 as a general introduction demands the keeping of wisdom – here represented as the priestly *tôrâ*. The admonition is then motivated by a promise of life (typical of the *tôrâ* – cf. Deut 8 1 30 16 and I Kings 3 14).

The introduction is followed by a positive, thematical explication (v. 3–10) of the religious character of wisdom teaching (as *tôrâ*!). The first topic concerns the religious recognition and social acceptance of the individual in obtaining *ḥɛsɛd wɛʾɛmɛt* (v. 3 + v. 4). The second and third topics are more personal, concerning personal belief (v. 5 + v. 6) and modesty (v. 7 + v. 8). Each of these units is motivated by a positive promise.

Verses 11–12, which concerns the topic of suffering, obviously forms the climax of the poem. The repetition of *bĕnî* and the content of v. 11 shows clear reference to v. 1. The primary intention of this poem is to indicate that if one is able to accept all good things from God, one must also be prepared to accept suffering from God. This final admonition is then causally (not with a promise!) motivated, referring to the father-son relationship[102].

The logical coherence and increased intent of v. 1 and v. 11–12 are obvious. But also within the poem itself one finds a sequence of cultic (and social), religious behaviour and personal religious (ethical) behaviour.

We may indicate the structure as follows:

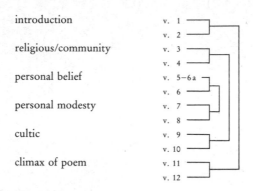

introduction	v. 1
	v. 2
religious/community	v. 3
	v. 4
personal belief	v. 5–6a
	v. 6
personal modesty	v. 7
	v. 8
cultic	v. 9
	v. 10
climax of poem	v. 11
	v. 12

Prov 3 27–35

The detailed description of the value, function and meaning of the wisdom in Prov 3 13–20 is followed by an admonition (v. 21), demanding the personal acceptance of wisdom. It is then motivated by a promise (v. 22–24). A sequence of admonitions (in Vetitive forms) occur in the following passage (v. 27–35), concerning the behaviour towards the poor and fellowmen (v. 27–30) and the wicked (v. 31). The motivation (v. 32–35) is introduced causally by *kî* and climactically finalized with a promise (v. 35). We may indicate the structure as follows:

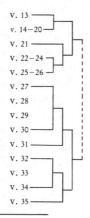

v. 13
v. 14–20
v. 21
v. 22–24
v. 25–26
v. 27
v. 28
v. 29
v. 30
v. 31
v. 32
v. 33
v. 34
v. 35

---

[102] It remains a task for scholars to determine the development of such a personal understanding of one's relation to Jahweh.

Prov 4 20–27

The extraordinary sequence of admonitions in this passage requires comment.

The passage begins with a general admonition to listen to wisdom counsel. It is motivated by a predication of wisdom's validity (v. 20–22). Then follows the central admonition (v. 23a – keep watch over your heart!)[103] which is causally motivated (v. 23b). In v. 24–27 it is made evident, by means of further admonitions, in which sense the heart must be guarded. Thus, we find a structure in which the cardinal theme (v. 23) figures in the centre of the composition:

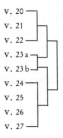

v. 20
v. 21
v. 22
v. 23a
v. 23b
v. 24
v. 25
v. 26
v. 27

A comparable structure is to be found in Prov 6 1–5 in which an accumulation of admonitions is found preceding and following the central theme (v. 3b). The typically casuistic introduction, which specifies the circumstances in which the admonitions are real, is the only difference.

Prov 5

Each chapter of Prov 1–9[104] consists of various poems, as is evident from the preceding discussion. The individual sayings and admonitions are structurally linked. This structure is of exegetical importance, because it is not only the smaller units that create the larger poem, but it is also the larger concept (structure) which determines the various units. Chapter 5 is such a well-rounded poem and together with Chapter 8 it is an artistic creation with exceptional qualities. The view of J. Schmidt which rejects any attempt to reconstruct complete poems in the wisdom literature, must therefore be entirely mistaken[105].

Chapter 5 as a poem glitters with literary and poetic devices such as homoio-katarkton, homoioteleuton, chiasm, paronomasia, symbols, etc. The poem begins with an introductory admonition: pay attention to my wisdom! Next follows a final clause (v. 3) as motivation and not a causal clause or a promise. Then, curiously enough, a predication (as motivation)

---

[103] Cf. Kayatz, C. op. cit. 43–47 on the topic of *lēb* in the wisdom texts.

[104] Compare the analysis of the various units in the study of C. Kayatz already referred to.

[105] Cf. Schmidt, J. op. cit. 32. Cf. also Baumgartner, W., TR 5 (1933), 272ff.

of the *zārâ* follows (cf. v. 3–6), without repetition of the initial demand. Here again the »strange« woman figures in stark contrast with wisdom.

In v. 7–8 follows a sequence of admonitions, directly related to the predication of the »strange« woman and her fatally seductive powers. These admonitions are then motivated (v. 9–14) by stressing the negative consequences of keeping company with the »strange« woman. In contrast with this negative explication, a positive admonition follows, metaphorically formulated: sexual satisfaction must be sought with one's real wife (v. 15). It is directly preceded by a motivation, formulated as a rhetorical question (v. 16–18a). Verse 18b is a connected admonition (have pleasure in your first married wife!) with its own motivation (v. 19–20) in the form of a predication of the real married wife of one's youth (again metaphorically highlighted).

In other words, in v. 3–6 and v. 9–14 we encounter a predication of the *zārâ*, which is then negatively explicated by means of admonitions and negative consequences. In v. 15–20 we have just the opposite order: First the positive admonition (v. 15–18a) and then the positive predication of the wife of the youth (v. 18b–20). The structural parts are therefore chiastically arranged.

The whole poem is artistically concluded by the predominant motivation (v. 21–23). The motivation is in the form of a result-description. The ultimate ontological judgement on man's behaviour and the result of his crooked ways in the eyes of Jahweh form the culminating point of this poem. The coherence of verses are represented diagrammatically on page 63.

We encountered a similar structure in Prov 1 10–19. Comparable structures are also to be found in Prov 6 20–35 and Prov 7 but the examples discussed are enough to show that larger poems exists in Prov 1–9 and that in particular cases a deliberately chosen structure is followed. Without recognition of the major structure, the contextual functioning of the individual admonitions and sayings will be in jeopardy.

Whereas we documented the isolated admonition in the previous analysis, we tried here to emphasize the structural and thematical unity of poems. The particular isolation of admonitions in Prov 1–9 was only a methodological differentiation.

3.1.13   Admonitions without Motivations?

Prov 23 12

Verse 12 would indeed cause us some trouble if we try to isolate it from verses 13–14. McKane[106] maintains the separation of v. 12 and v. 13–14, because the pupil is addressed in v. 12, whereas the father or apprentice

---

[106] McKane, W. op. cit. 385.

Chiastic structure

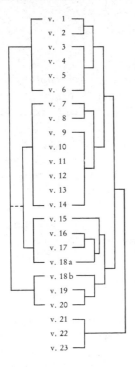

teacher of wisdom is addressed in v. 13–14. This suggestion sounds rather strange, because semantically v. 12 is related to v. 13–14. In v. 12 and v. 13–14 the pupil (whoever he might be!) is addressed. For what reason should the »pupil« apply his heart to instruction and his ears to wise advice? The answer is: Do not withhold discipline from a boy, because by means of discipline you put him on the right way and save his life from destruction.

There is not enough reason to detach v. 12 from v. 13–14 for the sake of maintaining the 30 sayings classification (cf. Amenemope and Prov 22 20). And also, if the classification of 30 sayings is maintained, there exists no criterion to exclude v. 12 semantically from the rest of v. 13–14. The compiler did not work without a sense of semantical categorization.

Comparable structures are present in v. 19–21 and v. 22–25: as general exhortations v. 19 and v. 22 cannot be isolated from the following context in v. 20–21 and v. 23–25 respectively.

Verses 12–14 must therefore be considered as a structural unity[107] in which v. 14 is to be understood as a motivation for both v. 12 and v. 13.

---

[107] Postel, J. op. cit. 108 totally ignored v. 12 in connection with v. 13–14.

Prov 27 2

yĕhallɛlkā zār wĕlō'-pîkā
nokrî wĕ'al śĕpāteͤkā
Let flattery come from a stranger, not from yourself,
from the lips of an outsider and not from your own. (NEB)

The sentence can be interpreted as an indicative or as an admonition. However, even if an indicative translation is preferred, the admonitory character remains fully present. The Jussive of *hll* therefore makes very good sense. Does this saying as a real admonition then exist without any motivation? A motivation, verbally explicit, is lacking. That, however, does not imply the total absence of any motivation. The antithetic character of this saying reveals an inherent motivation. The admonition is positively formulated: Let the stranger flatter you! The application of *wĕlō'-pîkā* which follows, not only contrasts with the first saying, but also the reason for the demand in the first saying: A wise man does not flatter himself. Against the background of the ethos of modesty[108] in the wisdom literature, this motivation (which is only partially explicit) becomes comprehensible.

Prov 31 8–9

There is no doubt as to the structural[109] and semantical coherence of v. 8 and v. 9. The admonition (v. 8 + 9) consists of three Imperative forms. The subordination by means of the *waw* and a secondary Imperative (v. 9b) is to be considered as the motivation and not as part of the admonition. The admonition of v. 8 is repeated in v. 9, but is then particularised with *śĕpāt-ṣɛdɛq*: Open your mouth and pronounce just verdict so that the poor and needy get their due[110]. The importance of the motivation is achieved by the imperative form in ordinary subordination, instead of an ordinary final clause, introduced by the *waw*.

The young king's *mišpāṭ* must be in *ṣɛdɛq*, so that he might be the patron of the poor and the needy. His judgement of the underprivileged according to the *ṣɛdɛq*-sentence is in harmony with the ethics of a wise king (cf. Prov 25 2.4 29 4 29 14 16 10 20 8 20 26 20 28 31 4–5 and 8 15–16).

The discussion made clear that no admonition in Proverbs exists without any motivation, although some might not be verbally explicit[111].

---

[108] Cf. Prov 8 13 11 2 11 20 16 5 16 18–19 17 19 18 11–13 21 4 21 29 22 4 26 12 29 23 and 30 11–14.
[109] Cf. the homoiokatarkton as poetic device and the chiastic rhythmic pattern: v. 8: 3+4

v. 9: 4+3

[110] Cf. McKane, W. op. cit. 260.
[111] Compare the classification of admonitions without motivations in Zeller, D. op. cit. 22.

3.2 Form-Critical Conclusions:

3.2.1 Index of References from Proverbs

Admonitions in the rest of the wisdom literature and in other biblical literature[112] were excluded from the preceding discussions. The form of the admonition and its motivative clause have been anal
index of references and structural features might clarify the conclusions to follow:

Reference	Coll.	Form of Admonition.	Form of Motivation.
16 3	B	Impt. (1)	Final Clause in *waw* + Impf.
22 6	B	Impt. (1)	Final Clause in *gam* + Impf.
22 10	B	Impt. (1)	Final Clause in *waw* + Impf.
9 9a	A	Impt. (1)	Final Clause in *waw* + Impf.
9 9b	A	Impt. (1)	Final Clause in *waw* + Impf.
20 13a	B	Vetit. (1)	Final Clause in *pen* + Impf.
19 20	B	Impt. (2)	Final Clause in *lemaʿan* + Impf.
22 24–25	C	Vetit. + Prohib.	Final Clause in *pen* + Impf. and *waw* + Perf.
25 8	E	Vetit. (1)	Final Clause in *pen* + Impf.
26 4	E	Vetit. (1)	Final Clause in *pen* + Impf.
26 5	E	Impt. (1)	Final Clause in *pen* + Impf.
25 9–10	E	Impt. + Vetit.	Final Clause in *pen* + Impf.
25 16	E	Impt. (1)	Final Clause in *pen* + Impf.
25 17	E	Impt. (1)	Final Clause in *pen* + Impf.
30 10	F	Vetit. (1)	Final Clause in *pen* + Impf.
30 8–9	F	Impt. + Vetit. + Jus.	Final Clause in *pen* + Impf.
31 4–5	H	Vetit. +Impt.	Final Clause in *pen* + Impf.
9 8a	A	Vetit. (1)	Final Clause in *pen* + Impf.
5 7–14	A	Impt. + Vetit. + Impt. + Vetit.	Final Clause in *pen* + Impf.
5 1–2	A	Impt. (2)	Final Clause in *lĕ* + Inf. Cstr.
7 1–5	A	Impt. + Jus. + Impt. (2) + Impt. + Jus.	Final Clause in *lĕ* + Inf. Cstr.
22 20 (?)	C	*hălōʾ*	Final Clause in *lĕ* + Inf. Cstr.
20 13b	B	Impt. (1)	Final Clause in Impt.
31 3	H	Vetit. (1)	Subordinate Clause in *waw* + NS
31 8–9	H	Impt. (3)	Subordinate Clause in *waw* + Impt.
31 6–7	H	Impt. (1)	Subordinate Clause in Impf.
19 25a	C	Jus. (1)	Subordinate Clause in *waw* + Impf.

---

[112] Cf. e. g. Qoh 7 9.10.16.17.21 5 1.3.5.7 10 20 10 4 8 2–4, etc. Sir 1 26 4 1ff. 4 20ff. 5 1ff. 6 1ff. 7 1ff. 8 1ff. 9 1ff. 10 6 11 2ff. 11 23 11 29 12 1ff., etc., Ps 27 9 38 22 40 18 44 24 49 17 37 1 7 2 13 4 28 1 50 22 59 12 74 19, etc., Ex 3 5 23 1.7 I Sam 1 16 9 20 16 7 2 3 Num 16 5 Gen 21 17 21 12, etc.

Reference	Coll.	Form of Admonition.	Form of Motivation.
19 25b	C	Impt. (1)	Subordinate Clause in Impf.
24 17–18	C	Vetit. (2)	Subordinate Clause in *pɛn* + VS
19 18a	B	Impt. (1)	Result Clause in *kî-yeš* + Impf.
19 18b (?)	B	Jus. (1)	Result Clause in (Motiv. 1st)
27 11	E	Impt. (2)	Result Clause in *waw* + Kohort.
24 15–16	C	Vetit. (2)	Result-description in *kî* + Vs
24 19–20	C	Vetit. (2)	Result-description in *kî* + VS
24 21–22	C	Impt. + Vetit.	Result-description in *kî* + VS
24 11–12	C	Impt. + Vetit.	Result-description in *kî* + VS
23 12–14	C	Impt. + Vetit.	Result-description in *kî* + VS
23 19–21	C	Impt. (2) + Impt. (1) + Vetit.	Result-description in *kî* + VS
23 10–11	C	Vetit. (2)	Result-description in *kî* + VS
8 32	A	Impt. (1)	Result-description in beatitude
8 33–36	A	Impt. (2) + Vetit. (1)	Result-description in *kî* + VS
6 25–26	A	Vetit. (2)	Result-description in *kî* + VS
29 17	E	Impt. (1)	Result-description in *waw* + Impf.
23 17–18	C	Vetit. (1)	Result-description in *kî-'im* + VS
22 26–27	C	Vetit. (1)	Result-description in *lāmmâ*
24 13a	C	Impt. (1)	Causal Clause in *kî* + VS
24 1–2	C	Vetit. (2)	Causal Clause in *kî* + VS
23 9	C	Vetit. (1)	Causal Clause in *kî* + VS
27 1	E	Vetit. (1)	Causal Clause in *kî* + VS
27 2 (?)	E	Jus. (1)	Causal Clause in antithetic paral.
22 22–23	C	Vetit. (2)	Causal Clause in *kî* + VS
26 25	E	Vetit. (1)	Causal Clause in *kî* + VS
27 13	E	Impt. (2)	Causal Clause in *kî* + VS
3 11–12	A	Vetit. (2)	Causal Clause in *kî* + VS
25 21–22	E	Impt. (2)	Causal Clause in *kî* + VS
23 1–3	C	Impt. + *waw* Perf. + Vetit.	Causal Clause in *waw* + NS
4 1–2a	A	Impt. (2)	Causal Clause in *kî* + VS
4 13	A	Impt. + Vetit. + Impt.	Causal Clause in *kî* + VS
4 23	A	Impt. (1)	Causal Clause in *kî* + VS
6 20–23	A	Impt. + Vetit. + Impt. (2)	Causal Clause in *kî* + VS
7 24–27	A	Impt. (2) + Vetit. (2)	Causal Clause in *kî* + VS
8 10–11	A	Impt. (1)	Causal Clause in *kî* + NS + VS
24 28	D	Vetit. (1)	Causal Clause in *waw* + Interrogative *ha*
22 22	C	Vetit. (1)	Causal Clause in Secondary demand
14 7	B	Impt. (1)	Predication in *waw* + NS
23 31–36	C	Vetit. (1)	Predication in VS
4 1 + 2b–9	A	Impt. (2) + Vetit. (1)	Predication in *kî* + VS

Reference	Coll.	Form of Admonition.	Form of Motivation.
4 14–19	A	Vetit. (2) + Impt. + Vetit. + Impt. (2)	Predication in *kî* + VS
4 20–22	A	Impt. (2) + Vetit. + Impt.	Predication in *kî* + VS
5 1–6	A	Impt. (2)	Predication in *kî* + VS
6 6–8	A	Impt. (3)	Predication in *ʾăšer* + VS
1 8–9	A	Impt. + Vetit.	Predication in *kî* + VS
1 15–18	A	Impt. (2)	Predication in *kî* + VS
8 5–9	A	Impt. (2) + Impt.	Predication in *kî* + VS
23 26–28	C	Impt. + Jus.	Predication in *kî* + VS
23 6–8	C	Vetit. (2)	Predication in *kî* + VS
23 4–5	C	Vetit. + Impt.	Predication in Interrogative + Simile
27 23–24	E	Impt. (2)	Predication in *kî* + Simile
5 18b–20	A	Impt. (1)	Predication in Simile
22 28	C	Vetit. (1)	Predication in *ʾăšer* + VS
27 10	E	Vetit. (2)	Predication in Popular proverb
5 15–18a	A	Impt. (1)	Predication in VS + Rhetoric Question
24 29	D	Vetit. (1)	Predication in Factual-description
20 19	B	Prohib. (1)	Predication in Popular Proverb
20 18	B	Impt. (1)	Predication in Popular Proverb
17 14	B	Impt. (1)	Predication in Popular Proverb
23 22–25	C	Impt. + Vetit. + Impt. + Vetit.	Predication in VS
24 14	C	Implicit Adm.	Predication in Mataphor
22 17–19	C	Impt. (2) + Jus.	Predication in *kî* + Jus.
1 23	A	Jus.	Promise in *waw* + VS
3 5–6	A	Impt. + Vetit. + Impt.	Promise in *waw* + VS
3 9–10	A	Impt. (1)	Promise in *waw* + VS
3 21–24	A	Vetit. + Impt.	Promise in *waw* + VS
3 1–2	A	Vetit. + Impt.	Promise in *kî* + VS
4 4	A	Jus. + Impt.	Promise in *waw* + VS
4 10	A	Impt. (2)	Promise in *waw* + VS
7 2a	A	Impt.	Promise in Impt.
4 5–6a	A	Impt. (2) + Vetit. (3)	Promise in *waw* + VS
4 6b	A	Impt. (1)	Promise in Impt.
3 3–4	A	Vetit. + Impt. (2)	Promise in Impt.
8 33	A	Impt. (1)	Promise in Impt.
9 5–6	A	Impt. (2) + Impt. (1)	Promise in Impt.
24 27	D	Impt. (2)	Conditional Clause

3.2.2 Structural Features of the Admonition as such in the Various Collections

In comparison with the number of proverbs in the various collections, the frequency of the admonition is the highest in Coll. C. Whether it is a result of Egyptian influence, we will discuss later. The majority of these admonitions are formulated in double stichoi in Coll. C., whereas they are normally single in Coll. B. and E. (the older wisdom). The majority of admonitions in Coll. C. are formulated negatively, whereas the majority of admonitions in Coll. B. and E. are formulated positively.

The majority (21) of proverbs in Coll. A. are also formulated positively. An interesting feature however, is the occurrence of positive and negative formulations within the same admonition (eg. Imper. + Vetitive). This kind of admonition is totally lacking in Coll. B. and occurs only once in Coll. E. But on the other hand it is frequently used in those collections with a more explicitly educational aim, namely Coll. A. and C.

The admonitions in Coll. A. normally consist of two stichoi or are more membered.

The admonition can be positively formulated by an Imperative or Jussive or negatively formulated by a Vetitive or Prohibitive. Positive and negative forms may occur within the same admonition. Absolute no distinction can be made between the positive (Imperative) and the negative (Vetitive) formulations[113]. The occurrences of the so-called Prohibitive form in Proverbs (cf. Prov 22 24–25 and 20 19) do not introduce a new genre (cf. Richter), but is stylistic variation of the one genre – the admonition.

It is further noteworthy that only one of the 13 admonitions in Coll. B. occurs in Chapters 10–15. Whether this fact is an indication of a more pronouncedly educational character latent in Chapters 16–22 17, is still to be proved. Whether this factor might play a role in the systematization of topics in Chapters 16–22 17 is also uncertain. It is, however, evident that Chapters 16–22 17 has a more »logical« arrangement of topics than Chapters 10–15[114].

3.2.3 The Motivative Clauses

Not one admonition in Proverbs occurs without any motivation. The motivative clauses are usually introduced with *kî, pɛn, waw, lĕ* . . . (+ Inf. Cstr.), *gam, lĕmaʿan, kî-yēš, ʾăšɛr*, or with a secondary verbal clause in the form of a simile (metaphor), popular proverb or even with a secondary Imperative or an interrogative particle.

---

[113] Cf. Zimmerli, W. op. cit. 185.

[114] A major task still lies ahead to determine in which way structural or semantic features are implemented to arrange various topics in the different collections.

When the admonition is formulated positively, preference is given to the *waw* and *kî* as introductory particles of the motivations. When negatively (or pos.-neg.) formulated, preference is given to *kî* and *pɛn* as introductory particles of the motivation.

Again it is to be noticed that also the motivations (compare the admonitions) in Coll. C. are, as a rule, double-membered and longer than those of Coll. B. and E. The motivations in Coll. E. are, as a rule, longer than those of Coll. B. In Coll. B. only two two-membered motivations occur while in Coll. E. more than 50% of the motivations are longer than single-membered sentences.

The motivation in Coll. D. is normally short and parallelistically arranged with a short admonition. In Coll. F. and H. the division between long and short admonitions and motivations is fifty-fifty.

In Coll. A. the motivations (except the promises) are long, mainly due to detailed predications.

According to our classification of the motivations, the following can be stated:

a) The motivations in final clauses are introduced with *waw, gam, lĕmaʿan, pɛn, lĕ* . . . and *hălōʾ*. In Coll. E., F. and H. only *pɛn* is used. In Coll. A. the introductory particles vary. Almost 60% of the final clauses in the various Collections are introduced by *pɛn*.

b) The motivations in subordinate clauses only occur in Coll. C. and H. and are normally introduced by the copula *waw*.

c) The *result clause* or result-descriptions as motivations are normally introduced by *kî* and are most frequently used in Coll. C. In these admonitions the Vetitive form dominates.

d) Motivations in causal clauses are frequently introduced by *kî* (only 3 exceptions). No preference of the Imperative (Pos.) or Vetitive (Neg.) can be determined in these admonitions.

e) The predication as motivation seems to be the most popular. The occurrences increase in those collections with an explicitly educational character (cf. Coll. A. and C.). The predication obviously became more popular in the younger wisdom literature[115]. It often occurs that an ordinary popular proverb or metaphor is used as predication.

f) The motivation in the form of the promise occurs only in the younger wisdom of Coll. A. The motivations as promise is normally introduced by the copula. Four occurrences, however, are explicated in secondary Imperatives.

All these admonitions concentrate around Jahweh (2) or the personified wisdom. These motivations reflect prophetic, priestly and deuteronomistic influences.

---

[115] Attention will be given to this aspect later.

g) Only one motivation (24 27) can be maintained as a conditional clause.

3.2.4 Form-Critical Development

It must be emphasized that we are operating with *one* genre, the admonition, which might be formulated with various imperative forms (Impt., Jussive, Vetitive and Prohibitive)[116]. These forms are stylistic variations of the admonitions and not new genres[117]. It is therefore impossible to maintain the Impf. + *lô'* (Prohibitive) in the wisdom literature as if it constitutes a typical genre proper to the stipulations of the law. It is a distinctive genre in lawsuits, but in the wisdom literature it is but one possible variation of the admonition. It is therefore incorrect to suggest a preferred position for the Prohibitive form at the expense of the Vetitive form[118]. Nevertheless, the Vetitive as composed with the Imperative (Pos.) form, is not to be seen as the original form of the admonition. There is no basis for the construction of such a hierarchical system built on stylistic variations.

W. Richter made an outstanding study of the occurrences of the admonition in the Old Testament and is correct in claiming that the admonition itself is a typical form of human speech[119] and might even occur in narrative literature. It is, therefore, difficult to relate the admonition, in general, to a certain life-setting. Richter failed to relate the admonition to a certain type of literature[120] and failed to describe it accordingly.

A further incomprehensible feature occurs in Richter's study, namely that he accepts the form of Prov 22 17ff. as original. Having análysed all the occurrences of the admonition in the various documents of the Old Testament, the logical conclusion would have been to maintain an admonition of the single imperative form (pos. or neg.) with a single motivations as original (cf. eg. I Sam 9 20 16 7 or occurrences in Coll. B. or E.). The best possible derivation of the form of the admonition, implies an extension of the basic form of the two-membered admonition. Why then should he maintain the four-stichoi forms in Coll. C. as non-Israelite in origin?

The differences of Coll. C. in comparison with Coll. B. and E. (shown in the preceding index of classification) were already noticed by Franz Delitzsch in his commentary on Proverbs in 1873, even before the Egyptian

---

[116] Compare Richter's view, op. cit. 190.
[117] Cf. Murphy, R., CBQ 31 (1969), 481.
[118] Cf. Richter, W. op. cit. 182.
[119] Ibid 67.
[120] Cf. Hermisson, H. op. cit. 85.

Instructions of Amenemope was made known in 1923[121]. The motivation is most frequently introduced by *kî* or *pen* which strengthens the dissuasive character[122] of this collection and it might be classified as *Instruction*.

Richter, however, declares categorically that the dependence of Coll. C. on Egyptian influence can be established from the linguistic structure of the admonitions in Coll. C. as compared with the rest of the wisdom literature. Egyptian influence[123] may be present but cannot be proved from the linguistic structure of the admonitions. Such attempted proof implies an apriori acceptance of Egyptian influence: Are the four-stichoi forms in Coll. E. and A. also results of Egyptian influence? The *parallelismus membrorum* as the dominant stylistic feature in Hebrew poetry seems to have played a major role right from the beginning of the literary fixation of wisdom in the form of admonitions.

An over-estimation of the »Instruction« as genre at the expense of the admonition is found in the study of McKane[124]. The individual admonitions in the different collections are also treated as »Instruction«. The larger instructive units (such as Prov 1—9) might be classified as »Instruction« but it is still composed of various literary genres such as the admonition. And therefore the admonition as such cannot be identified with the larger structure (Instruction). A metaphor is not an epic, because the metaphor operates in the epic!

The greater frequency of the admonition in the »Instructions« of the later wisdom literature (cf. Prov 1—9 and Sirach), does not necessarily indicate an evolutionary development from the single admonition[125]. The primary fact of frequency of the admonition in later wisdom literature is evident, but this frequency must also be seen in the light of the content and intention of the »Instruction«, not only as a natural development, realized in linear time (evolution). The frequent use of the admonition can also be ascribed to the ingenuity of the sage or teacher in making the dissuasive element of his teaching more effective. The more »academic« and educational character of the wisdom teaching, makes the admonition a natural choice! Therefore, we reject the term development in this regard, because it embodies unwarranted assumptions.

The previous analysis claims to prove the coherence of admonition-motivation in all the collections. The motivation is an integral part of the

---

[121] Cf. his Biblical Commentary on the Proverbs of Solomon, 1872, I 16ff. and Vol II 95ff. Cf. also Gemser, B. op. cit. 83.

[122] Cf. Postel, J., op. cit. 136.

[123] Cf. Brunner, H., Handbuch der Orientalistik, I 1952, 90ff.; Kayatz, C. op. cit. 135ff.; Lang, B., Die weisheitliche Lehrrede, 1972; McKane, W. op. cit. 6ff. and 262ff.; Hermisson, H.-J. op. cit. 84.

[124] McKane, W. op. cit. 3.7.263 etc.

[125] Richter, W. op. cit. 47.

admonition. This assumption is maintained over against those scholars who consider the motivation to be a later development — determined by a pedagogical life-setting[126]. The oldest admonitions in Proverbs present themselves in combination with motivations. This coherence must, therefore, be considered as original[127].

3.2.5   Linguistic Description of the Admonition

We have already shown (cf. Par 2.2.13) that the admonition and wisdom saying (Aussage) are the two elements of the Sentence. Contrary to the indicative mood of the wisdom saying, the admonition is formulated with an imperative (positive or negative in a Vetitive or Prohibitive form). The admonitory element of the admonition is always followed by a motivative element. The admonition as a natural form of speech finds its basic functional setting in the educational institutions. But, in form it always transcends the boundaries of pedagogical speech.

In both Gerstenberger's and Richter's analysis of the admonition, an indefensible disdain of the motivative clause occurs to the detriment of the imperative element. Such a simplified working model enables both scholars to compare legal prohibitions and wisdom admonitions. Two basic assumptions of Gerstenberger's and Richter's method remain problematic: that the motivation is a secondary element can be doubted, and that the admonition can be described purely linguistically is questionable because it presupposes a dualism between form and content. Bjørndalen[128], therefore, seems to be correct when he exposes Richter's inconsistency in attempting to provide a strictly grammatical description of the admonition. The terminology, as descriptive elements, however, reflects semantical categories which emerge from the content of the admonition. Bjørndalen's criticism[129] is directed against the priority given to the form[130] of the admonitions by Richter. Form and content[131] cannot be divided in an atomistic manner in genre-description. According to Bjørndalen descriptions such as »Vetitive«, »Imperative« and »heischendes Präsens«[132] first become relevant as a result of the semantic content. Taking the content into

---

[126] Cf. von Rad, G. op.cit. 122 and Richter, W. op.cit. 190.

[127] Our following discussion on the form-content relation and the role of the motivation will illuminate this coherence more explicitly.

[128] Bjørndalen, A. J., ZAW 82 (1970), 348ff.

[129] The background of Bjørndalen's criticism is to be found in the study of the Dutch structuralist, A. Reichling, Das Problem der Bedeutung in der Sprachwissenschaft, 1963.

[130] Cf. also the criticism of Stoebe, H. J., ThZ 25 (1969), 59.

[131] Cf. Koch, K., Was ist Formgeschichte?, 1974, 3—21 and 289—342. Compare also Hermisson, H.-J. op.cit. 58 and 84f. and von Rad, G. op.cit. 31—40.

[132] Richter, W. op.cit. 37ff.

consideration, Bjørndalen then goes so far as to extend Richter's description of the admonition by adding descriptive elements, which he calls »Deixis ad oculos« and »Anaphorische Deixis«[133]. This approach must be rejected. By entitling every form of immediate structure and semantic dependence in the wisdom admonitions as new descriptions, the categories of Bjørndalen could well be extended. Recognition must be given to aspects of content, but too many descriptive features would only provide an unwieldy definition. We could therefore suggest a more general definition which does not necessarily explicate every linguistic and semantic feature.

Adopting the traditional assumption of the »Gattungsgeschichte«[134], which correlates a specific form of speech with a special speech content, Bjørndalen maintains that a comparative analysis of the speech *topoi* will enable one to extract the constitutive (»gemeinsame«) aspect of the wisdom admonition. Certain objections, however, must be raised. The wisdom literature has a preference for certain *topoi*, but the real character of the admonition cannot be determined only from the uniformity of topics treated in the wisdom literature. The unity of the *topoi* does not centre in their semantic relatedness only, but mainly in their function and purpose within the genre of the admonition. One would not grasp the main purpose of the wisdom admonitions by comparing the semantic values of the *topoi*. The intention[135] of the admonition within the wisdom literature provides the constitutive element which integrates and directs the use of *topoi*. An apriori understanding of the intention of the admonition is also impossible. The content of the *topoi* reveals the incidence and particular explication, but not necessarily the dominant intention. We are therefore compelled to distinguish between the intention of an utterance in a certain context and the intention of the genre within the corpus of wisdom literature. To be more exact: The admonition of Prov 23 10–11, followed by a direct motivation, prohibits the removal of boundary stones. The motivation stresses the intention of the admonition. But why is this admonition motivated as it is? Why is this specific transgression so prominent in the wisdom literature? The immediate context cannot provide this answer and hence one must appeal to the primary intention of the wisdom admonitions as a whole.

Therefore we maintain the unity of form and content, because the form itself is already a certain expression of knowledge of reality. The content is without intention and scope when separated from the form and its functioning.

---

[133] Bjørndalen, A. J. op. cit. 359.

[134] Cf. Bernhardt, K. H., Die gattungsgeschichtliche Forschung am AT als exegetische Methode. Ergebnisse und Grenzen. 1956, 34 ff.

[135] Cf. Hoffmann, H. W., ZAW 82 (1970), 341–346.

I suggest the following definition: The admonition consists of an admonitory element, in the grammatical form of an Imperative, Jussive, Vetitive or Prohibitive and a motivative element, which might vary in grammatical form, length and explication. The introductory particles of the motivative clauses vary and cannot necessarily be connected to the positive or negative character of the admonitory element. (*pɛn* seems to prefer a negative introduction).

The *parallelismus membrorum* seems to be the dominant principle of structural arrangement. The form and length of the admonition do not necessarily develop in an evolutionary way and cannot always be contributed to external influence. Didactic implementation, differences in background and different social language contexts might have structural influences.

3.2.6 The Relation of Admonition and Wisdom saying (Aussage)

From our analysis of the admonition it has appeared that the form of the admonition is linguistically distinctive of the wisdom saying[136]. The admonition gives preference to the imperative mood (or relevant mood) whereas the wisdom saying is formulated in the indicative mood. The *parallelismus membrorum*, as the linguistic explication of the traditional symmetry of thought, is normally constructed in the wisdom saying in co-ordination and in the admonition in sub-ordination. The admonition always consists of a motivative clause, whereas the motivative clause very seldom occurs within an ordinary wisdom saying. In a number of instances, however, the subordinate member of the saying functions as a motivation (cf. Prov 13 14 15 24 16 12 14 27 21 7 22 2 22 9 29 19 24 5–6 and 22 29).

The frequent use of the admonition in the later wisdom literature (except Coll. C.) has led to the assumption of a development of the wisdom saying into the admonitory saying. Zimmerli says thus: »Es darf also für Formentwicklung des Maschals von Prov 10 ff. bis zu Prov 1 ff. wohl von einem Stilwandel hin zum Mahnspruch, zum Gebotspruch geredet werden.«[137] Proof of such a development is claimed to be found in those admonitions which could easily be transformed into wisdom sayings (cf. Prov 16 3 20 13 25 16 25 17 25 21 26 4–5) and vice versa (cf. Prov 10 20 and 10 3)[138]. Hermisson also speaks of »Übergangsformen«[139].

As stressed earlier, the admonition and wisdom saying must be maintained as the two elements of the Sentence (mashal). Absolutely no indication has been found to support a theory of development. The

---

[136] Cf. the analysis of the wisdom saying by Hermisson, H.-J. op. cit. 141 ff.

[137] Cf. Zimmerli, W. op. cit. 186. Cf. also Zeller, D. op. cit. 23 and Gerstenberger, E. op. cit. 120.

[138] Ibid. 184.

[139] Hermisson, H.-J. op. cit. 160 f.

popularity of the admonition in the later wisdom literature[140] depends on the life-setting, the function and the intention within a certain genre.

The maintenance of so-called »Übergangsformen«, such as Prov 20 16 (27 13), cannot be supported without an intolerable separation of form and content. Hermisson, e.g.[141], failed to prove that Prov 20 16 is not an admonition nor did he show how it suits the genre of the wisdom saying. Admonitions which occur together with wisdom sayings in the same proverb (cf. Prov 28 17 and 17 14) are no proof of transition either. In these cases the wisdom sayings are the substantial motivations.

To maintain the development-theory, and to relativize the authority of the admonition[142], minimizes the peculiarities of the admonition and wisdom saying. The coherence in content of the admonition and the wisdom saying should be recognized, but that in itself does not allow us to make statements about the authority (see later), nor does this coherence abolish the structural and intentional differences between these two genres. The content and intention determine the form.

The ethos (see later) expressed in the wisdom saying and the admonition cannot be distinguished absolutely. Noteworthy is the fact that, as a rule, the ethos is not embedded in the admonitory part of the admonition, but in the motivation. The content of the motivation normally correlates with the ethos of the wisdom saying. Hence an understanding of the coherence of admonition and motivation is extremely crucial (see later on the role of the motivation).

The differentiation in genre does not necessarily mean the rejection of similarity between the ethos of the wisdom admonition and the wisdom saying[143]. Thus, we are inclined to differ with Westermann[144] who exaggerates the difference between wisdom saying and admonition. The admonition as such, might have an original setting outside the wisdom tradition, but the existence of the wisdom admonition in the wisdom literature cannot be held to be a secondary feature. A possible co-existence of these two genres in the wisdom literature cannot be rejected simply on the ground that the function of both forms might originally have been distinctive. This distinction in function is also emphasized by Von Rad: »Während die Mahnung dem Hörenden eine ganz bestimmte Handlungsweise nahelegt, haben die Aussagesätze, so markant sie sich geben, doch immer eine eigentümliche Offenheit, etwas über sich Hinausweisendes, das den Raum für vielerlei Assoziationen freigibt, ja unter Umständen sogar auch eine

---

[140] In Qohelet the admonition occurs sparsely.
[141] Hermisson, H.-J. op. cit. 161.
[142] Zimmerli, W. op. cit. 187.
[143] This unity is also recognized by Zimmerli, W. op. cit. 186.
[144] Westermann, C., Weisheit im Sprichwort in: Gesammelte Studien II, 1974, 153.

bildliche Ausdeutung nicht verwehrt.«[145] A functional difference exists, but that does not mean a different origin nor that the ethos expressed by both is different. In the admonitions the truths (ethos) of experienced reality are combined with specific demands, which actualize that ethos in prescriptions to the individual. The »general« ethos (also expressed in wisdom sayings) is now made relevant to the conscience of specific persons, (pupils, sons, court officials, etc.). For this very reason the admonition always anticipates the motivation which must make clear why it is so essential to obey the demand. The wisdom saying reveals the truth in itself and anticipates no further explication. This ethos of the wisdom saying is not »neutral« in the sense of no call to obedience even though the formulation may appear to be neutral, for lack of appeal to specific persons. The indicative formulation does not conceal the latent demand. It is the general ethos, whose acceptance would be reflected in every aspect of human behaviour. The admonition makes this demand patent by relating a certain truth to a certain form of behaviour (which does not necessarily mean that it is the only application of that truth).

To conclude: Structurally the wisdom admonition must be distinguished from the wisdom saying. That, however, does not mean that the ethos expressed in the one is incompatible with that of the other. There is no substantial evidence for the development of the wisdom admonition from out of the wisdom saying. They exist side by side (cf. Prov 16 1–3). Again it is the content and intention which also determine the structure.

3.3 The Life-Setting (Sitz im Leben) of the Wisdom Admonitions

The form-critical approach has opened up a vast and problematic field of study in attempting to determine a genre's life-setting[146]. We must again determine the value of this method in view of the measure of support found for such a theory within the genre itself.

Biblical and rabbinic traditions ascribe the growth of wisdom tradition in Israel to the Israelite court — beginning with Solomon. And there is no reason not to believe it. The creation and development of a state administration presupposed able and skilled personnel as well as institutions for their education. Fohrer even maintains a sort of court wisdom as in Egypt[147]. The establishment of the monarchy might even have given rise to various schools of education in which the wisdom literature also functioned[148].

---

[145] Von Rad, G. op. cit. 48.
[146] Cf. the Criticism of Buss, J., ZAW 90 (1978), 157–171, on the approach of H. Gunkel to tradition.
[147] Fohrer, G. op. cit. 337.
[148] Cf. Scott, R. B. Y., VTS 3, 1955, 262–279; Zimmerli, W., ZAW 51 (1933), 180;

Scholars who are opposed to this »class-setting«, normally lay emphasis on the family as the original life-setting of the wisdom sayings[149]. According to J. L. Crenshaw, the wisdom originates in the family »and from the period of the clan ethos derive many of the proverbs whose purpose was to equip one for the mastering of life, regardless of circumstance«[150].

More prominence to the family as life-setting of the wisdom, and particularly the wisdom admonitions, is given by the study of E. Gerstenberger[151]. He denies an absolute distinction between the so-called Prohibitive form (lō' + Impf)[152] and the Vetitive form ('al + Jussive). Except for a few cases, according to Gerstenberger, the prohibitions and admonitions totally lack any reference to Jahweh as subject or the cult as a basic premise. He concludes: »Die Mischung von Autorität und Vertrauen auf vernünftige Überzeugungskraft, die Art und Weise, eine einsichtige, überschaubare Ordnung sichern zu wollen, die wir bei den Prohibitiven meinten feststellen zu können, führen uns dazu, eine *patriarchalische Institution* als Autorität hinter den Verboten zu suchen und nicht eine staatliche oder priesterliche«: (cf. p. 60—70). Thus the family becomes the life-setting of the so-called apodictic laws and wisdom admonitions (cf. p. 110—113).

W. Richter[153], through an extensive analysis of the Prohibitive and Vetitive in the Old Testament, comes to a conclusion, quite opposite to Gerstenberger's. Thus, the prohibitive forms of the law and the wisdom admonitions originate in certain social groups which could be called schools (priestly and wisdom)[154]. These »Gruppen« would have been the authoritative institutions and as such the very origin of this tradition.

In an attempt to evaluate these two main solutions, one has to appreciate the importance of both the family and the school. They were, in fact, the most important institutions in ancient Israel[155].

Beaucamp, E., Man's Destiny in the Books of Wisdom, 1970, 4—7, and Mettinger, T. N., Solomonic State Officials, 1971.

[149] Eichhorn, J. G., Einleitung in das Alte Testament, 1824⁵, 72 ff., already laid emphasis on the family as the circle in which the wisdom developed. Cf. also Whybray, R. N., BZAW 115, 1974, 15 ff. 54 and 69—70; Audet, J-P., Origines comparées de la double tradition de la loi et de la sagesse dans le proche-orient ancien, 25th International Congress of Orientalists, 1960, 352 ff.

[150] Cf. his essay in Old Testament Form Criticism (ed. Hayes, J. H.), 1974, 227.

[151] Wesen und Herkunft des apodiktischen Rechts, 1965, 60 ff. and 110 ff.

[152] Cf. Alt, A., KS I, 1952, 289—332.

[153] Loc. cit.

[154] Ibid. 117.

[155] Cf. Dürr, L., Mitteilungen der Vorderasiatisch-Aegyptischen Gesellschaft 36/2, 1932, 67 ff.; Brunner, H., Altägyptische Erziehung, 1957, 41 ff.; Hermisson, H.-J. op. cit. 81 ff. and 113 ff.; Crenshaw, J. L. op. cit. 227 ff., and Andersen, F. I., The Bibl. Transl. 20 (1969), 37.

Important, however, in any grammatical analysis of a genre, is the distinction between the form itself, which might have applicability outside the specific genre, and the function of that form, as the vehicle of particular content, in a specific genre. The prohibitive and admonition might be elements of everyday lingual usage. But the admonition (e.g. the wisdom admonition) anticipates an exact tradition and in this sense it would, in principle, be possible to determine more concretely the life-setting of the wisdom admonitions. To shift forms back to archetypes of human speech, contributes little to our attempt to understand genres[156].

The main problem, of both Gerstenberger's and Richter's contribution, is that both emphasized the linguistic form of the admonition unduly at the expense of the content. The life-setting of a genre cannot be determined by the linguistic form alone. Other features (see later) have to be considered.

Gerstenberger and Richter ignored the motivative clause of the admonition (or explained it as a secondary appendage) so that only the imperative sentence is taken as a working model, thus facilitating comparison with the law code. Thus the admonition is connected with the law code but it finds no appreciation within the wisdom tradition as such, nor does it do jutice to the coherence of admonition and wisdom saying (Aussage).

To solve the problem and to avoid exclusive reference to either the school or the family, by synthesizing the two, will not help either. According to this position, the wisdom originates in the family, but eventually serves didactic purposes in different schools[157]. The schools indeed do play a major role[158], as stressed before, nevertheless, the school is not the sole life-setting.

---

[156] Cf. the fundamental criticism of Wagner, V., Rechtssätze in gebundener Sprache und Rechtsatzreihen im israelitischen Recht, 1972, 58, and Liedke, G., Gestalt und Bezeichnung alttestamentlicher Rechtssätze, 1971, 19−61, on Gerstenberger.

[157] Cf. Hermisson, H.-J. op. cit. 88.

[158] Lang, B., Die weisheitliche Lehrrede, 1972, 100, has pointed out that Prov 1−9 is »school literature« which correlates in characteristics with the same literature of Egypt. Cf. also Kayatz, C. loc.cit.; Munch, P., AO 15 (1937), 112−140; Thompson, J. M., The Form and Function of Proverbs in Ancient Israel, 1974, 80 ff.; Olivier, J. P. J., JNSL 4 (1975), 49−60; Wiseman, D. J., JNSL 5 (1977), 77−91, and Klostermann, A., Schulwesen im alten Israel, in: FS Th. Zahn, 1908, 193−232. The latest article on this subject, from B. Lang, Schule und Unterricht im alten Israel, in: La Sagesse de l'Ancien Testament, 1979, 186−201, convincingly establishes the fact of existing schools in Israel and also demonstrates to what extent the wisdom literature reflects its educational character.
About the Mesopotamian schools: Cf. Kraus, F. R., Vom mesopotamischen Menschen der altbabylonischen Zeit und seiner Welt, 1973, 21 ff.; Falkenstein, A., WO 1 (1948), 172−186; Kramer, S. N., JAOS 69 (1949), 199−215; Gordon, E. I., JAOS 74 (1954),

Collections of wisdom sayings originate in these schools, but this collecting and systematizing activity is not to be seen as a mechanical process. The creative spirits of sages, priests, teachers, etc. were at work in this process. In Qohelet, Sirach, Job and Prov 1—9 the creative hand of the compiler cannot be ignored.

The proper method for determining the life-setting would be to trace the ethos-related ethics of each saying. I do not imply that the ethos of any one social group, e.g. the family, remained restricted to just the family or that cultic ethos applied exclusively to the priestly and prophetic circles. The schools in their didactic function might well have honoured such an ethos. Hence one should not try to see all domestic illustrations in the wisdom for emulation or shunning as belonging only to the family ethos[159]. The »domestic illustrations« for instance, provided by Qohelet are purely reflective of a cosmic understanding of Qohelet's existence within the one reality (allowing for no discrepancy between world experience and belief). They are not determined by a family ethos.

Thus, although the ethos expressed in a certain saying cannot be strictly limited to a certain institution, the only method for determining the initiating institution(s) of the ethos expressed in the saying, is to analyse and compare the topics and ethos of the particular sayings. In this regard the admonition cannot be treated apart from the wisdom saying.

Accordingly we are confronted with:

a) *A family ethos* in Prov 10 1 15 20 17 25 19 13 19 18 19 26 12 1 13 1 21 9 21 19 23 12—25 27 11 29 15, etc. These sayings reveal the value of obedient recognition of the parents' instructions. The family ethos is not only concerned with the orderly functioning of the family, but the family must also be in orderly and righteous co-existence with its surroundings, the community and Jahweh (cf. Prov 11 9 12 7 16 8 21 3 21 15 28 5, 10 3 15 9 and and 17 15). In this sense the family must reflect the order at large.

In the circle of family education ordinary experienced wisdom (even in popular proverb form) might have played an important role. It might even have occasioned the causal attachment of certain consequences to particular acts of behaviour (cf. Prov 17 19 17 20 18 16 19 9 19 13 19 24 20 17 21 25 22 6 22 8, etc.). I would suggest that this traditional act-consequence »dogma« is not merely a result of educational and cultic (official) circles, but correlates with the cosmic experience of the orderly sequence of nature's events. It is experienced wisdom which enables comparison (and even identification) of human features with that of nature (cf. e.g. Prov 17 12 10 25 14 4 17 3 23 4—6

82—85; Gese, H. op. cit. 66f. and Oppenheim, A. L., Ancient Mesopotamia, 1964, 228—289.

With regard to the Egyptian schools: Cf. Brunner, H. op. cit. 13 ff. and Dürr, L. op. cit. 6 ff.

[159] Crenshaw, J. L. op. cit. 227 ff.

26 1 26 2 26 11 26 20 27 17, etc.). Man's understanding of his existence as part of ordered reality would necessarily be jeopardized if there were no coherence between his conduct and conduct's consequences.

We might also assume that the family wisdom is incorporated in the didactic material of the various institutions of the court-centred administration. That does not mean that it does not also continue as family wisdom. Rather, it continues as such side by side with the developing educational institution.

b) *A school ethos*[160] in traditional topics of wisdom such as the contrast between the wise and the foolish (cf. Prov 12 15.16 13 1 14 8 14 16, etc.), the wise woman and the wicked woman (cf. Prov 14 1 12 4 31 10ff., Chapter 9 etc.), the poor and the wealthy (cf. Prov 10 15 14 20 13 18 13 11 17 5, etc.), the willing and the sluggard (cf. Prov 19 15 6 9–11, etc.), etc. The ethos of modesty (cf. Prov 12 9 16 19 19 17 29 23, etc.) and wise counsel (cf. Prov 10 19.20.21 12 23 17 7 11 11 11 12, etc.) might also have been popular topics. But still it remains very difficult to determine an exact school ethos, for the school was the place in which various sayings were collected. The ethos represented in these sayings is not necessarily the achievement of the school officials only. Major parts of the proverb collection (cf. the wisdom teachings in Prov 1 — 9) may be ascribed to the schools if the focus is only on the structural thematization and literary form. The ethos of the school education did not contrast with the family ethos, but represented it *in loco parentis*[161].

c) *An official (court) ethos*[162] in Prov 31 3 31 4–5 31 6–7 24 11–12 24 27 24 28 24 29 25 8 25 9–10 11 14–15, etc. Official administrative topics such as just weights (Prov 11 1), sound administration (Prov 11 14), position of the king (cf. Prov 31 4 28 16 29 14 25 6, etc.), juridical aspects (Prov 16 10 17 9 17 10[163] 17 15 17 18 21 28 18 5 18 17, etc.), etc. are familiar topics. The words of Lemuel (31 1–9) reflect a typical court ethos. It is also interesting that the majority of proverbs in Chapters 28—29 (in distinction from Chapters 25—27) reflect a court ethos.

The court ethos is concerned with the orderly functioning of the administration, social justice and the official position of the ruler[164]. Tra-

---

160 Although the school is first mentioned in Sirach 51 23, the prior existence of such an institution can be determined from the character of the wisdom literature and in comparison with school literature outside Israel; Cf. B. Lang loc. cit. and Wolff, H. W., Hosea, 1965², 122.

161 Cf. from the author, JNSL 5 (1977), 59.

162 II Sam 16 23 Prov 25 1ff. and the prologue of Achiqar make us aware of this educative function of the king's court. Cf. also de Boer, P. A. H., VTS 3, 1955, 42ff., and Thomson, J. M., The Form and Function of Proverbs in Ancient Israel, 1974, 9.

163 Cf. Erman, A., Die Literatur der alten Ägypter, 1923, 244.

164 Cf. Brunner, H., Gerechtigkeit als Fundament des Throns, VT 8 (1958), 428.

ditional wisdom topics, such as the control of the tongue, also find a place in the court educational material[165].

The view which takes the king's court to be the representative par excellence of orderly (including social) existence, makes the attribution of collections of sayings to court functionaries or kings comprehensible.

d) *A pristly ethos* in Prov 13 14 13 20 18 10 28 4 28 7 30 8 30 10 3 1–12, etc. This ethos is mainly concerned with the sacral law and cultic obligations. Here it becomes necessary to distinguish between experienced wisdom and theological wisdom, because under priestly influence a tradition emerged which in the end identified wisdom and priestly *tôrâ* (consequently in Sirach). This distinction does not, however, mean that the experienced wisdom is non-religious.

e) *A prophetic ethos* in Prov 1 20–33. From this passage it becomes evident that even the prophetic circles have influence on the wisdom and that these two traditions cannot be absolutely isolated from each other (certainly not in the post exilic period).

f) *An individual ethos* in Prov 30 1–9[166]. This passage with its lamenting character reminds us of Job and the Psalms (cf. Ps 73)[167]. We have every reason to believe that this passage originates from an individual devout person or sage.

Hermisson also points out certain proverbs (Prov 10 15 13 8 14 10 14 20 18 23 19 4.6.7) which most likely were initiated by the experience and reflection of an individual, rather than by a family ethos[168]. The individual indeed might figure as the initiator of a wisdom ethos even before a family ethos arose. The inhabitant of the Ancient Near East experienced his existence within a reality in which features and activities do not form a total chaos, but are part of an ontological order. Not only natural features reveal a regularity, but also human existence in its interrelatedness with the cosmos of which it is an integral part. The pattern of human behaviour therefore might be in harmony or in conflict with its ontological order (cf. the unity of phenomena of nature and of human existence in Prov 25 16 25 23 26 20). A particular deed is not a neutral activity, the result of the accomplished act, but it has effects and consequences in as far as the act itself is in harmony or in conflict with the created order, (cf. Prov 11 2 and

---

[165] Cf. Kayatz, C., Einführung in die alttestamentliche Weisheit, 1969, 27.

[166] Although Prov 30 1–14 is classified as the words of Agur (cf. LXX), verses 1–9 reflect a distinctive character from the rest. Cf. also Kovacs', B. W., Is there a Class-Ethic in Proverbs, in: Essays in Old Testament Ethics (ed. J. L. Crenshaw), 1974, 173–189, objections against the popular assumption that the wisdom literature is school literature. He suggests that it must be seen as a »stylized form of intellectual reflection« (p. 187) which stresses the importance of the individual.

[167] Compare also the Babylonian Dialogue of Pessimism, in Lambert, G., BWL, 1960, 148 ff.

[168] Hermisson, H.-J. op. cit. 52 ff.

26 27). The result of this understanding of existence was the systematizing
of experiences and features. Comparison of human behaviour with features
of nature might originate in the individual's experience of the natural world,
(cf. Prov 27 8 15 17 and 27 5). It is conceivable that this experienced wisdom
of the individual might have become articulated in elementary didactic
sayings, which eventually found their way into the family and school
educational systems.

It seems therefore necessary to maintain an individual ethos, which
cannot however, be isolated precisely.

In conclusion we may say:

a) The sayings in Proverbs do not represent a uniform ethos − even if
all the literature might be evaluated as school literature!

b) The literary form of the admonition is no direct indication of what
the life-setting might be.

c) To determine the life-setting of the wisdom admonition the wisdom
saying must be taken into account.

d) If a single life-setting of the wisdom sayings is to be formulated, it
must be a comprehensive one to accommodate the differentiation of ethos
as here discussed. In this regard the *Israelite city*[169] seems to meet the
requirements. The Israelite city, the cultural, religious and educational
centre, as life-setting enables the maintenance of the diversity of ethos
which we encountered in Proverbs. The mutual influences of the various
social groupings evident in the sayings presuppose geographical proximity.

A major task for future scholarship would be to determine in which
way and to what extent the various intellectual and educational institutions
influenced each other in the Israelite city. It would also be important to
trace the processes of amalgamation which eventually gave rise to the school
of the Synagogue in the post-exilic period.

---

[169] Cf. Fuss, W., Tradition und Komposition im Buche Jesus Sirach (Diss. Tübingen), 1962,
289.

Chapter 4: The Ethos of the Wisdom

In this chapter our aim is to discuss some of the findings of our preceding enquiry in view of an interpretation of the admonition. This is a vast and complicated field and we therefore restrict ourselves to certain aspects which will illuminate the ethos of the admonitions. We cannot begin to discuss the impact of the ethos of the wisdom admonitions on human conduct and belief, for the simple reason that it has not yet become clear what this ethos is. According to the conditions laid down in our method of approach, our main concern is with the motivation. Much has already been said on the role of the motivation in the preceding chapter, but not enough to evaluate its importance for our understanding of the ethos.

4.1 The Role and Function of the Motivation

At first it must be made clear that the motivative clause does not occur only in the wisdom literature, but also in lawsuits[1] and in the prophetic sayings[2].

In the prophetic literature the prophetic word is promulgated as the word of God and normally motivated with reference to the active God and his righteousness and with reference to the history of salvation of Israel (Heilsgeschichte).

In the lawsuits and *tôrâ*-teachings of the Pentateuch the motivation often refers to Israel's history of salvation (especially in Deuteronomy and the Book of the Covenant): often with reference to the proclamation of salvation and disaster; reference to the sacredness of Jahweh and the people of Jahweh (cf. the so-called Sacred Law) or the sacredness of certain institutions and objects (cf. the Priestly Code) and with reference to the social order (mainly in the Book of the Covenant and Deuteronomy)[3].

Contrary to the frequent explicitly religious and sacred history motivations in the lawsuits and prophetic sayings, the absence of sacred history motivations and the relatively small number (11) of explicitly religious motivations following the admonitions are remarkable. This could

---

[1] Cf. Gemser, B., VTS 1, 1953, 50—66, and Rücker, H., Die Begründungen der Weisungen Jahwes im Pentateuch, 1973.

[2] Wolff, H. W., ZAW 52 (1934), 1—22.

[3] Cf. Rücker, H. op. cit. 39—93 in this respect.

lead one to think of Jahwistic re-interpretation[4], especially with reference to Collection C with its supposed parallel in the Egyptian Instructions of Amenemope. If Jahwistic re-interpretation is undertaken to establish the religious character of the sayings, then serious objections must be raised, for then one must suppose that the basic premise in wisdom thought concerning all aspects of order, is not transcendental. In other words it is supposed that social ethics (e.g.) and religion are separable. Such dualism did not exist in the Ancient Near East, however. The explicit reference to Jahweh in Proverbs might well be functional within a new framework of religious reference.

It is further necessary to look more closely at those admonitions in which an explicit religious motivation occurs. The tradition of a theological wisdom, worked out in Prov 1−9, would obviously bring wisdom in relation to Jahweh − as demonstrated in the climax of Prov 8 33−36. The acceptance of wisdom's *tôrâ* would mean religious acknowledgement (by God) and social acknowledgement (by fellow men) − cf. Prov 3 3−4.

It is noteworthy that in all the other occurrences of explicitly religious motivations (not only in Collection A), reference is made to the patronage of Jahweh with respect to the created order. It is Jahweh who regulates human conduct (Prov 16 3 and 3 5−6) and even human suffering (Prov 3 11−12). It is Jahweh who is the patron of the social order[5] (cf. Prov 22 22−23 23 10−11 24 17−18 and 25 21−23), the juridical order (cf. Prov 24 11−12) and the religious order (cf. Prov 23 17−18).

The frequency of explicit references to Jahweh is pro rata the highest in Collection C. Does this constitute a deliberately attempted Jahwistic re-interpretation in order to distinguish these sayings from their counterpart in Amenemope? Or are these references determined by the inherent intention and content of the sayings?

Although a few admonitions concerning the cult do occur in Coll. A. (cf. Prov 6 20−23 and 3 9−10), no motivation refers to the cultic order. Quite a number, however, are motivated with reference to the priestly *tôrâ* or sayings normally connected with the *tôrâ* (cf. Prov 3 1−2 3 9−10 4 4 4 5−6 6 20−23 and 7 2a).

Not one admonition in Proverbs is motivated with reference to the history of salvation. The social order only appears sparsely in the motivation. As is to be expected, it only occurs in Collections which centre around the official court such as Coll. C (cf. Prov 23 1−3 and 22 28) and Coll. H (cf. Prov 31 3 31 4−5 and 31 8−9). The vast majority of motivations (77%) are motivated with reference to experience and logic. Although it is

---

[4] According to Gerleman, G., OTS 8, 1950, 15 ff., the explicitly Jahwistic motivations in the later wisdom literature can be determined from a tradition-historical point of view.

[5] Cf. Fensham, F. C., JNES 21 (1962), 129−139; AION 31 (1971), 160, and Nel, P. J., JNSL 5 (1977), 61−63.

experienced wisdom, one cannot classify it as purely prudential[6], as if no religious aspect is concerned. We find the categories of »religious« and »prudential« insufficient to describe the variation of thought in the motivations. These categories presuppose an unacceptable dualism.

It has already been noted that the sequence of admonition-motivation in Proverbs is a fixed structural feature. The motivation does not occur regularly in the law or other priestly or prophetic sayings. The occurrence of the motivation, together with the wisdom saying is also limited to a small number of proverbs[7]. It must, however, be stated that the number found by Postel[8] can be increased considerably, because Postel looks exclusively for grammatical features to be convinced of a motivation. The semantic aspect is largely ignored. In this respect the parallel structuring of sentences deserves more attention. Only extensive study of this aspect might prove to which extent the second phrasemember of a wisdom saying manifests a motivative relation to the first member. In Prov 25 5 the second stichos obviously fulfills the function of a motivation. A comparison might also embody an implicit motivation, cf. Prov 25 14.18.19.20 26 1.3.7.8.9.11 and 18−19. This co-ordinative arrangement of comparable features constitutes an inner logic in which emphasis is laid not only on the comparable peculiarities, but also on the apriori of symmetry. In other words, what makes it possible and to what extent and for what purpose are different things comparable? What inner logic makes it possible to compare the snow in summer with the honour of a fool (Prov 26 1)? Is the cosmic contradiction (snow in summer!) not also an implicit motivation for an even greater anomaly − honour showed to a fool!?

The few notes above suffice to make one aware of a possible implicit motivative element, even in the wisdom sayings without structural indications. However, the motivation never functions so prominently in the wisdom saying as in the admonition.

The question thus arises, why is the admonition always followed by a motivation? The popular answer is invariably for didactic purposes[9].

It is well true that the motivative clause might be of importance in an educational situation as a means for effective explanation. It appeals to comprehensibility. It elucidates, declares and makes the experienced truth relevant in its direct admonitory character. In this sense it helps the listener to discover the truth and worth of instruction. Thus, it is indeed a valid didatic instrument!

But, it could not be proven that the motivation was indeed a later addition to the admonition as a result of its functioning in school-context.

---

[6] Cf. Oesterley, W. O. E., The Book of Proverbs, 1929, xiii.
[7] Stated before in par. 3.2.6.
[8] Postel, J. op. cit. 84, 133.
[9] Cf. Postel, J. op. cit. 178−181.

On the contrary we found that the admonition and motivation co-exist from the very beginning. This assumption forces us to look, quite apart from its didactic function, at the inherent constitutive logic which determines the coherence. Hence again we are confronted with the impossibility of separating form and cotent in an atomistic manner.

In the wisdom literature we are encountered with man's first endeavour to order knowledge of experience and to formulate the order of empiric observation in comprehensible gnomic sayings. With this attempt comprehensible knowledge of the created order is made available. This process is, however, not one of abstract speculation. No, it is the recognition of inherent laws of order and an attempt to reveal them in a cognitive sense. Man is obliged always to accept this knowledge, because it constitutes orderly human conduct.

The admonition demands orderly human conduct and the connected motivation reflects the experiences of inherent natural laws[10]. This wisdom not only includes the perception of the logical consequences, but also, inevitably, confrontation, because this wisdom is knowledge of the created order and therefore of God himself[11].

The motivation is therefore not only a didactic device or logical principle, but it is directed towards the ethos of human conduct.

In contrast with the stipulation of the ethical decalogue, the admonitions do not promulgate the created order by means of absolute regulations, but demand acceptance of the created order by means of their conclusive illumination of this order. The admonition as such is no absolute rule, because it has so little persuasiveness. However, in combination with the motivation, the admonition makes evident in which respect the created order must be constituted also in the particular act of human conduct. The admonition in Prov 24 17 (e.g.) does not say much without the motivation in verse 18. In other words, the form and logic of the admonition already anticipate a motivation! For this very reason it is unacceptable to maintain the motivation as a later invention of educational circles.

The way in which the motivation is connected with the admonition to illuminate the truth and validity of the admonition, which mainly aims to make the created order comprehensible and imperative for human existence, differs. The motivation reveals this truth in various ways[12]:

a) By means of its *reasonable character* it appeals to one's reason, in referring to empirical verifiable observations and to accepted religious truths which have originated in an existence devoted to Jahweh (cf. e. g. Prov

---

[10] Cf. von Rad, G. op.cit. 90—92.

[11] We will return to this point later.

[12] Compare the classification of Postel, J. op.cit. 140—170.

3 11–12). This is achieved by connecting the motivation causally to the admonition[13].

The admonition is constructed in such a way that when a negative topos (anything irregular or against the created order) occurs in the admonitory part, then it is motivated causally with reference to the distinctiveness of the negative *topos*, cf. Prov 8 25–26 22 26–27 22 22–23 23 9 23 20–21 and 24 1–2. On the other hand, if the admonition implies a positive prescription, then it is positively motivated (cf. e. g. Prov 3 11–12 8 33–36 13 20a (?) 23 12–14 23 17–18 and 29 17. There are only three exceptions in Coll. C. (cf. Prov 22 22–23 23 10–11ʳ and 24 11–12). In all three the admonition is negative, but the motivation refers positively to Jahweh's justice.

b) By means of its *dissuasive* character in which the final consequences and results of one's behaviour are illuminated[14]. When these motivations are closely examined, one clearly gets the impression that the majority originate in the act-consequence (»Tun-Ergehen«)[15] dogma, a typical phenomenon of the earlier wisdom. The following assumption plays a major role: The wise knows the way of the righteous, and the wicked has it in himself to reveal his wickedness in the act itself or in the outcome of the evil act. By experience and observation of the wicked, the distinction between the righteous and the wicked becomes plain to the wise[16].

c) By means of its *explanatory* character, which consists of a predication of what is demanded[17]. This is probably the most striking category in which the function of the motivation is best expressed. The credibility and authority of the admonition originate in an appeal to observation. It is therefore conceivable that this type of motivation was the most functional form and apparently became more popular in the later wisdom literature. Why this form of motivation became more popular in a Collection such as Prov 1–9, is not easy to say. One might consider the possibility that the typical *topoi* of the wisdom were by now more defined and their symbolic and metaphoric functions were more »canonized«. The new theological re-interpretation of wisdom and its *topoi* might have added a further creative horizon. The predication of one of these *topoi* enables the listener to grasp the meaning of the prescription and, even more important,

---

[13] Compare our Index of References in par. 3.2.1.

[14] Compare the Index of References, par 3.2.1. about the final, result and subordinate clauses.

[15] Cf. Gese, H. op. cit. 33 ff. and 42 ff., Fichtner, J. op. cit. 25 and 62 f. and Skladny, U. op. cit. 89. For a brief look at the various assumptions, cf. Emerton, J. A. Wisdom, in: Tradition and Interpretation (ed. G. W. Anderson), 1979, 216–221.

[16] We will return to this point later.

[17] Cf. the Index of References, par. 3.2.1. under predication.

to understand the necessity to regulate his existence, according to the demand of wisdom, and not to deviate from it.

In the interest of clarity let one example be quoted from our classification: Prov 5 1–5. The demand to listen to the *těbunâ* of the wisdom teacher (?) is directly motivated by a predication of the *zārâ*. The predication of the *zārâ*, as *topos* of the wisdom, immediately makes clear that the *zārâ* has a certain connotation with symbolic significance. Otherwise it would be impossible for the *zārâ* to figure, without any explanation, as a motivation. The *zārâ* symbolizes more than the factual seductive woman. The *zārâ* becomes the epithet for all the evil represented by the *zārâ*. That is why it is possible for the sage to polarise the wisdom and the *zārâ* diametrically[18].

Understanding of the predication lends force to the meaning of the admonition without which it might be inadequately understood. No hearer can misread the motivative character of this predication when he raises the question »why?«.

d) By means of its *promissory* character the value of the wisdom becomes evident. The promise as motivation only occurs in Coll. A. The character of these motivations makes it almost impossible to deny prophetic and deuteronomistic influences (as already found in Prov 1 and 3). The promises as motivations are also concerned with a new concept of wisdom and wisdom teaching, in respect to the theological re-interpretation of wisdom. This new concept appears from the Persian period onwards. The gap between wisdom counsel and *tôrâ-commandments* is practically reduced. The frequent occurrence of the deuteronomistic promise of life, connected with wisdom's prescriptions, is therefore an almost natural phenomenon.

This promissory character of the motivation intensifies the call to obedience of wisdom's counsel, for wisdom is the wisdom of Jahweh and it is He who lengthens the prosperous and meaningful existence of those who intentionally devote their lives in harmony with this wisdom.

Consequently, one can say that the motivation is an irreplaceable structural element of the admonition. The main intention of the motivation is to illuminate the truth and validity of the admonition by means of its reasonable, dissuasive, explanatory and promissory character. The dominant dogmatic premise occurs to be that of the created order which in no way contradicts wise thought. The motivations shows to which extent the human act violates or honours this order.

---

[18] The *zārâ* evidently reflects an interesting development of tradition which is connected with a variable appreciation of the woman.

4.2   Authority in the Wisdom Admonitions

The authority of the wisdom admonitions (and of the wisdom literature as such) has not attracted as much attention as, e.g., the authority of the Law and the Prophets[19]. The main reason might be that the authority of the wisdom is not made verbally explicit. In many detailed studies one is struck by absence of attention to authority.

If the wisdom admonitions are characterised as utilitarian or eudaemonistic sayings[20], it is difficult to maintain an authority requiring obedience. Hopefully the stage of classifying wisdom as utilitarian, together with the negation of its religious character[21], is now past.

In recent research the accent has shifted to the »Gattungsgeschichte« as a means to determine the life-setting (Sitz im Leben) of the wisdom sayings. The particular life-setting is then also regarded as the authoritative institution which legitimates the validity and credibility of the wisdom sayings. In this regard E. Gerstenberger maintains the family (»patriarchalische Institution«)[22] as the »Sitz im Leben« of the wisdom admonitions. He denies an absolute distinction between the so-called Prohibitive form ($l\bar{o}$ + Impf.)[23] and the Vetitive form ('al + Jussive). The authority of these sayings (even in the law code) does not centre in an official state institution or a priestly institution, but in the family. The father of the clan or family then, is the authoritative person.

Although we do not deny the importance of the family and its function within the Israelite community[24], it is impossible to maintain that it is the only life-setting of the admonitions and in particular, it cannot be seen as the institution which sanctions the authority of the admonition. There exists no direct indication in Proverbs that the family or head of the family is regarded as fundamental to the authority of the wisdom. Even in Prov

---

[19] Cf. eg. Overholt, T. W., CBQ 41 (1979), 517–532.

[20] Cf. Baumgartner, W., Israelitische und altorientalische Weisheit, 1933, 27–29, and also Baumgärtel, F., Eigenart der alttestamentlichen Frömmigkeit, 1931, 38, and Zimmerli, W., ZAW 51 (1933), 194.

[21] The religious character is emphasized by Brunner, H., Handbuch der Orientalistik, II 1952, 95–109, De Buck, A., N.Th.T. 21 (1932), 322–349; von Rad, G. op.cit. 86ff.; Würthwein, E., Wort und Existenz, 1970, 201f., and Anthes, R. op.cit. 13 who points out the religious character of one of the oldest Instructions in Egypt, namely that of Ptaḥḥotep.

[22] Gerstenberger, E. op.cit. 60–70. A family-wisdom prior to a school-wisdom is already suggested in 1960 by Audet, J. P., 25th International Congress of Orientalists, Moscow, 1960, 352ff.

[23] Cf. Alt, A., KS, 1 1952, 289–332.

[24] Cf. our discussion in par. 3.3.

41–4, with reference to the family education of the wisdom teacher, the intention is not to stress the authority of the admonition by referring to the family. In this particular occurrence emphasis is laid on the authoritative character of the teacher who acts *in loco parentis*[25], but that itrself is not a motivation for the authority of the admonition as such.

It must be emphasized that no attempt is made to deny the authoritative character of the family and of family education, but that the admonitions for their authority should be linked with the authority of the family (-father), is to be questioned.

We have already pointed out[26] that W. Richter came to a totally different conclusion, although he applied the same method of the »Gattungsgeschichte«. According to Richter the Vetitive and the Prohibitive forms of the law and the wisdom admonitions originate in certain social groups which could be called schools (priestly and wisdom schools)[27]. The authority of these stipulations then centres in the authority by which they are promulgated: God, priest, prophet or teacher[28]. Although Richter does not maintain a class ethics explicitly, it is almost inevitable to come to such a conclusion because he restricts the ethic code exclusively to certain social circles[29].

Apart from our objections against the treatment and solutions for the lifesetting of the wisdom admonitions given by Gerstenberger and Richter[30], we must state categorically that the »Gattungsgeschichte« cannot provide the answer for the question of the authority of the admonitions. It is a very doubtful approach to relate the authority of the wisdom (-admonitions) to the authoritative character of the institution or functionaries of the presumed life-setting. No linear coherence exists between the life-setting and the authority of the wisdom admonitions. The authority of the admonitions does not originate in the authority (God, priest, teacher, etc.) by whom they are proclaimed.

How should we then define the authority of the wisdom admonitions? Could the structural form of the admonition itself be an indication of its authority? To our mind the only answer is to be found in the admonition itself and especially in the motivative clause connected to the admonition[31]. The

---

[25] Cf. from the author JNSL 5 (1977), 59f.

[26] Cf. par. 3.3.

[27] Richter, W. op. cit. 117f. and 140–145.

[28] Whybray, R. N. op. cit. 67 categorically denies any authority other than the authority of the teacher. The main purpose of the wisdom is the well-being of man (anthropocentric) and the teacher has the authority to establish what is desirable for man (68).

[29] Richter, W. op. cit. 182f.

[30] Cf. par. 3.3.

[31] In which way the admonition and the *tôrâ*-command are interdependent, will be discussed in the following sub-division.

authority originates in the truth of the wisdom expressed in the admonition[32]. Therefore we are inclined to maintain the coherence of admonition-motivation as due to the very nature of the admonition, its persuasiveness and its intention. This consistency of admonition-motivation is essential in trying to determine the authority of the wisdom. It is the motivative clause that provides the reader the authority. The admonition does not depend on an authoritative institution; even those admonitions explicitly religious, do not depend on God in a causal way. The admonition depends on its intrinsic truth, made explicit in its motivation. In which way this truth is illuminated by the motivative clause is explained in detail in the preceding paragraph.

However, the fact that no institution, in which the wisdom is endowed with authority and promulgated as such, could be determined, does not mean that the wisdom has in fact no authority. If one accepts institutional authority as the only form of authority, the disdain of wisdom's authority is conceivable. This assumption is clearly evident in Zimmerli's remark: »Von Weisheitsgebot im strengen Sinn kann nicht geredet werden. Der autoritäre Charakter fehlt der Weisheitsmahnung, ihre Legitimation geschieht nicht durch Berufung auf irgendeine Autorität.«[33]

Wisdom, according to Zimmerli is debatable ʿēṣâ, not straightforward legislation. The person addressed is made aware of certain experienced truths, which are stated in an impersonal way. In the active working of the experienced rules on man, Zimmerli found the motivation for man's obedience[34].

Zimmerli has every right to stress the importance of experience, but the authority of the wisdom cannot be reduced to man's response in confrontation with or in consideration of experienced rules. The objectives of wisdom are not neutral and they are not dependent upon man's response for their validity. It is the truth of the wisdom, expressed in the motivation, which comprises the imperative to obey the demand. The very nature of the motivation embraces an effective appeal to reason and observation, because the cosmic order and the ethical order are not contradictory. The wisdom expressed in the admonition represents the created order in which one's existence finds its destiny. The created order is comprehensible within the frame of the yirʾat Jahweh. Knowledge of this order is wisdom and this wisdom is embodied in sayings and admonitions. This knowledge therefore, does not represent intellectual facts, but an ethos through which an orderly (religious) existence is possible. This ethos is in fact revealed knowledge of righteous human conduct, and has an authority in itself apart from man's response to it.

---

[32] Even the wisdom saying (»Aussage«) must be considered in this respect.

[33] Zimmerli, W. op. cit. 187. Cf. also Schmidt, J. op. cit. 54.

[34] Zimmerli, W. op. cit. 182—187.

In order to illustrate our assumption that the authority originates in the truth of the wisdom of the admonition, new concepts are introduced which call for further attention and should make the conclusion more understandable. The understanding of the ethos of the wisdom is essential for the understanding of wisdom's authority. Before we get to a discussion of the ethos we have to take a brief look at the relation of the *tôrâ*-stipulation to the admonition and also at the connotation of *yir'at Jahweh* in Proverbs.

4.3 The Relation between the Tôrâ and the Wisdom Admonition

It is not our intention to engage in a detailed discussion of the form and function of the *tôrâ* in the Old Testament[35], but rather to show in which way the *tôrâ*-stipulations and the wisdom admonitions cohere in the wisdom literature, especially with a view to their interpretation.

The distinction in form between the wisdom admonition and the *tôrâ*-stipulation must be maintained. The Prohibitive form of the law has in itself an authoritative claim[36]. The wisdom admonition, as we have seen, always tries to explain or motivates. It is well-established that the motivations of some of the Decalogue stipulations are secondary developments[37]. If so, why should the admonition be linked with a motivation and not the law prohibition? We have ascertained that the wisdom admonition has an authority of its own which is spelt out in a typical wisdom manner.

Secondly, we are confronted with the fact that the law and the wisdom admonitions do not exist totally in ghetto's. Otherwise it would have been impossible to find a tradition in the Old Testament which identifies the law and wisdom[38]. Already in Prov 3 the wisdom is represented as the priest who proclaims the sacral law. The influence of the *tôrâ*-tradition on

---

[35] Cf. Gerstenberger, E. op.cit.; Richter, W. op.cit.; Wagner, V. op.cit.; Gemser, B. op.cit.; Kessler, W., VT 7 (1957), 1–16; Petuchowski, J. J., VT 7 (1957), 397ff.; Würthwein, E., ZThK 55 (1958), 255ff.; Zimmerli, W., Gesetz im Alten Testament, ThLZ 85 (1960), 481–498, and Das Gesetz und die Propheten, 1969, 7ff.; Kutsch, E., ZAW 79 (1967), 18ff.; Gese, H., Zur biblischen Theologie, 1977, 55ff.; Van Oyen, H., Ethik des Alten Testaments, 1967, 85ff.; Rendtorff, R., Die Gesetze in der Priesterschrift, 1954; von Rad, G., Theologie des Alten Testaments, I 1957, 193ff.; Liedke, G., Gestalt und Bezeichnung alttestamentlicher Rechtssätze, 1971; Pfeiffer, R. H., JBL 43 (1924), 294–310; Mowinckel, S., ZAW 55 (1937), 218ff., and Schmidt, W. H., VTS 22, 1972, 201–220.

[36] Cf. Richter, W. op.cit. 77ff. and Alt, A., KS, I 1953, 278–332.

[37] Cf. Stamm, J. J., ThRNF 27 (1961), 189–239 and 281–305; Mowinckel, S. op.cit. 218–235; van der Woude, A.S., De Thora in de Thora, 1967, 11ff., and the excellent study of Gese, H., Vom Sinai zum Zion, 1974, 61–80.

[38] Cf. Gese, H. op.cit. 68ff.; Marböck, J., BZ 20 (1976), 1–21; Kaiser, O., ZThK 55 (1958), 51–63; von Rad, G. op.cit. 316ff.; Schmid, H. H. op.cit. 150ff.; Hengel, M.,

wisdom becomes also more prominent in Prov 1–9 in as far as typically Deuteronomistic promises are attached as motivations to wisdom admonitions[39]. This development paved the way for the eventual identification of the law and wisdom in Sir 24. Already in Chapter 1 26 the gap between the law and wisdom is closed:

> v. 26: »If you desire wisdom, keep the commandments and the Lord will convey her to you.« (JB)[40]

Wisdom and law do not exist without relation to each other, but are interdependent. Chapter 17 11–14 provides another explanation of this interdependence when the author specifically refers to the giving of the law at Sinai (cf. Ex 19.20 and 24):

> v. 11: He set knowledge (wisdom) before them,
>   he endowed them with the law of life.
> v. 12: He established an eternal covenant with them,
>   and revealed his judgements[41] to them.
> v. 13: Their eyes saw his glorious majesty,
>   and their ears heard the glory of his voice.
> v. 14: He said to them, »Beware of all wrong-doing«,
>   he gave each a commandment concerning his neighbour. (JB)

And then in Chapter 24 the wisdom is finally identified completely with the law[42]. The detailed and majestic selfrepresentation of the wisdom (v. 1–22) is followed by verse 23:

> All this is no other than the book of the covenant of the most High God,
> the law that Moses enjoined on us,
> an inheritance for the communities of Jacob. (JB)

The question is now raised: What is the constitutive element in this identification of the law and wisdom? There must be a similarity in the very nature of the two which enables this tradition to reach completion. The

---

Judentum und Hellenismus, 1973, 284 ff., and Fuß, W. op. cit. 291 ff. etc.

It is impossible to determine the relationship between the *tôrâ* and wisdom only by a formal investigation into the use of the concept *tôrâ* in the wisdom literature, as Hudal, A., Die religiösen und sittlichen Ideen des Spruchbuches, 1914, 167 ff., attempts. He concludes that there is no formal congruence between the *tôrâ* and the wisdom and explains the identification of law and wisdom in Jesus Sirach as due to the new accent on the law under hellenistic pressure (183). The formal relatedness of *tôrâ* and wisdom is important, but also the intention of both and the development of these traditions.

[39] Compare our classification of the promises as motivations in par. 3.1.6.

[40] Compare also Sir 19 20.

[41] It refers to the Mosaic Law given at Sinai. Verses 13–14 describe this event.

[42] Compare also Ps 119 97–99 and Baruch 3 9–4 4 in which the *tôrâ* and wisdom are identified.

categorical definition of G. Kuhn[43], that the commandments order the relations towards God while the admonitions guide through a profane world, does not satisfy, because this definition minimizes the importance of the development of tradition up to Jesus Sirach. Secondly, it reflects a dualism between social ethics and religion.

The relatedness of the law and wisdom cannot be clarified sufficiently from a single life-setting as W. Richter and E. Gerstenberger intended[44]. The form is then absolutized on behalf of the content. It apparently occurs that the content and intention of the law and the wisdom are the impetus for the development of tradition. Richter's emphasis on the »Ethos«[45], expressed in both the law and wisdom can be appreciated. This shows his awareness of the relatedness of the two. One problem, however, arises when he declares: »Die Bezeichnung »Gesetz« oder »Recht« wird also dem Entstehen und Gebrauch der Prohibitive nicht gerecht, vielmehr stellen sie ein Ethos dar, das ein Verhalten in einer abgegrenzten Umwelt regeln will.«[46]

If the Decalogue-stipulations are also to be classified as »Prohibitive« (which seems to be the case), then certain objections must be raised against his disapproval of »Recht« as a qualification of the Decalogue. If the more detailed codification of the Decalogue is meant, then his formulation is acceptable. If the Decalogue as such is implied, one cannot go along with his point of view. The tôrâ is law (Recht) and ethos. If the tôrâ is only ethos, it becomes a goal in itself and a legalism is unavoidable. For if the tôrâ is only ethos, then it constitutes the relation of Jahweh and his people. This is in fact maintained by Baumgärtel: »Dieses irdische Leben wurde zergliedert in seine ganze Vielfältigkeit, und diese Vielfältigkeit wurde bezogen auf den göttlichen Willen . . . Nun braucht der Fromme nur in allen einzelnen Fällen die Gebote zu halten, und er hat den Weg zu Gott, er hat Gott selbst in dem Leben, das Jahwe, sich zu ihm bekennend, ihm schenkt.«[47] If this assumption is maintained, a religious optimism seems to be the logical consequence[48].

The relation between Jahweh and his people (Israel) does not originate with the Decalogue. The Decalogue is given because a relationship (a covenant) already exists between Jahweh and his people. The covenant does not depend on the law as its condition. The law is given within the context

---

[43] Beiträge zur Erklärung des Salomonischen Spruchbuches, 1931, 2f.
[44] Cf. our discussions in par. 3.3. and par. 4.2.
[45] Richter, W. op.cit. 140—145 and 190ff. This does not mean that we agree with his limitation of this ethos to a class-ethics.
[46] Ibid. 190.
[47] Baumgärtel, D. F., Eigenart der alttestamentlichen Frömmigkeit, 1931, 48.
[48] Ibid. 61.

of the covenant[49] and defines the salvation — the condition of the *šālôm* — reality[50]. The law delimits the *šālôm* in as far as it excludes chaos (evil). The negative formulation of the apodictic law is given by Würthwein as follows: »daß es nicht den Gewinn der Gottesgemeinschaft ermöglichen, sondern ihren Verlust verhindern will«[51].

The Decalogue is not a legal codex for the governance of court proceedings, but it is the provision of the law — the order of Jahweh. The Decalogue is the promulgation of God's order and therefore of God's will[52]. The law is the »gesamte Willensoffenbarung Jahwes an Israel«[53]. In the very full sense of the word this truth is formulated by H. Gese when he declares that the totality of the *tôrâ* is congruent with the totality of revelation[54].

From this very brief look at the law it should be clear that the Decalogue can be qualified as law (»Recht«)[55] in as far as it represents the order of salvation within the framework of the covenant. This law is explicated or codified variously in the Old Testament. The codification necessarily embeds an ethos, for now the individual in his concrete and personal existence is confronted with the revelation of God's will. Now that the meaning of the law has been stated, we must shed more light on the relation of the law to wisdom which, later, was to become a relation of identity.

---

[49] Von Rad, G., Theologie des Alten Testaments, I 1957, 196 ff.; Noth, M., Die Gesetze im Pentateuch. Ihre Voraussetzungen und ihr Sinn (Gesammelte Studien zum AT 6), 1957, 53 f.; Zimmerli, W., Das Gesetz und die Propheten: Zum Verständnis des Alten Testaments, 1969, 55 ff.; Eichrodt, W., Theologie des Alten Testaments, 1 1957⁵, 9 ff.; Fensham, F. C., Exodus in De Prediking van het Oude Testament, 1970, 117 ff.; McCarthy, D. J., Treaty and Covenant: A study in form in the Ancient Oriental documents and the Old Testament, 1963; McCarthy, D. J., Old Testament Covenant: A Survey of Current opinions, 1972; Nissen, A., Gott und der Nächste im antiken Judentum. 1974, 65 f.; Würthwein, E., ZThK 55 (1958), 266 f., has shown that the law cannot be separated from the covenant. An extremely critical attitude against the covenant's role in the Old Testament is expressed by Kutsch, E., Verheißung und Gesetz: Untersuchungen zur sogenannten »Bund« im Alten Testament, 1973.

[50] Cf. Gese, H. op. cit. 57 f. and ThLZ 85 (1960), 147–150, for his description of the apodictic laws which »gehört nicht zum Bereich des Rechts im Sinn der Rechtsfindung, des Richtens, als vielmehr zum Bereich der Rechtssetzung, der Ordnungskonstituier der Heilsgründung; es wird hier nicht gezeigt, wie gerichtet werden muß, sondern was Recht ist, es wird Ordnung, der heilvolle Zustand, es wird *šālôm* gegeben«.

[51] Würthwein, E. op. cit. 267.

[52] Cf. Deut 6 1

[53] Von Rad, G., Theologie des Alten Testaments, I 221 f.

[54] Gese, H. op. cit. 61.

[55] Against Richter, W. op. cit. 190.

Th. C. Vriezen[56] has correctly pointed out that from the phase of tradition in which Israel became more and more aware of the cosmic majesty of Jahweh and developed a Jahwistic cosmology, the problem of the relationship between the cosmic order and the will of God arose. In other words: What is the relation between the revelation of the created order and the order of salvation (revelation of God's will in the law)? Or very con-- cretely: What is the relation between reason and revelation (wisdom and law)? For the solution of this relationship, the most liberating concept was moulded in tradition, viz. wisdom and law are not contradictory, but the congruency of both constitutes *the* truth! The God who makes his will known to his people in the *tôrâ* is also the creator of this world[57]. The order of this creation is comprehensible to the created human being[58]. The sage is on the alert and observes this created order[59]. Within the framework of the *yir'at Jahweh* he reveals this order, most frequently crystallising it in the form of wisdom sayings. The created order is not a merely scientific object of wise reflections, but in the created order Jahweh reveals *the* order in which human existence finds its destiny. Accordingly the wise present this order as an ethos for human conduct.

On the one hand we have the categorial promulgation of the will of God in the law and on the other hand the revealed created order of Jahweh in the wisdom literature. The theological tradition could not possibly view the created order of Jahweh as if it existed apart from the law[60]. Theologically they have to give account of the relation between wisdom and the revelation of God's will. The only way to do so was to see the two in their identity: No dualism or contradiction exists — wisdom is possible in obedience to the law (Sir 1 26)[61]. The order demanded in the revelation of God's will is identical with the order which Jahweh bestowed upon the created universe. »Die *Tôrâ* wird zum einen Teil der universalen Weisheit Gottes, die in der Schöpfung grundgelegt ist.«[62]

---

[56] Vriezen, Th. C., An Outline of Old Testament Theology, 1966, 25 ff.

[57] M. Limbeck demonstrates satisfactorily in his study (Die Ordnung des Heils, 1970) that even the *tôrâ*-interpretation of early Judaism (2−1 century BC) reflects signs of adjustments to accommodate the belief in the created order of Jahweh (63 ff.). The *tôrâ* and the order of creation are uncontradictorily claimed to be of importance in reason and conduct (76 f.).

[58] Compare the remarks of Gese, H. op. cit. 174 on Ps 104 24 and Prov 3 19f.

[59] Cf. Von Rad, G., Theologie des Alten Testaments, I 1969⁶, 430 ff.

[60] Cf. Gese, H. op. cit. 69.

[61] We have paid attention to this identification in Jesus Sirach.

[62] Marböck, J. op. cit. 6. Cf. also Rickenbacker, O., Weisheitsperikopen bei Ben Sira, 1973, 88 f.

The order prescribed in the law does not differ from the created order. The order of God's will proclaimed in the law is explicated or codified in the wisdom[63]. This identity is to be deduced from the very nature of the wisdom and is not necessarily postulated under pressure of external factors[64].

The wisdom admonitions are the explicated ethos of the created order[65]. The wisdom admonitions as the admonitory explication of this ethos, intend to order human existence in harmony with the will of God. This wisdom which is accessible to man, is the wisdom through which God created everything (cf. Job 28 and Prov 8 22ff.)[66]. The wise and righteous man (ṣaddîq) desires and obeys this wisdom in his doings; his existence is in harmony with Jahweh's created order as revealed in the law. The wisdom is mediated to man by God as the foundation of real existence[67].

4.4 The Yir'at Jahweh

As indicated earlier, wisdom is an international phenomenon of the Ancient Near East and probably constitutes the first attempt in history at cognitive systematisation, which we could call scientific. It consisted of an evaluation of man's experience of the world and in the process led to the establishment of inductively derived principles of order governing the world and human conduct in it. Characteristic of all wisdom literature is that it attempts to explain cosmic and human features in terms of an order which penetrates and constitutes created reality. The question rises as to how this knowledge is justifiable theologically.

---

[63] The law as the proclamation of God's will or of God's law does not need any motivation, but the admonition in which this law is codified or in which the eternal law is represented as ethos is motivated to show in which way the obedience to the prescribed demand constitutes the will or order of God. It is possible, because reason is not necessarily in contradiction with revelation.

[64] Marböck, J. op. cit. 19 is attracted by the *nomos* and wisdom ideas of the Greek popular philosophers, which might have contributed to the identification of law and wisdom by Jesus Sirach.

[65] The coherence of the *tôrâ* and creation is also accepted as an important aspect of Christian ethics, cf. eg. Heering, H. J., Is er een eigen christelijke ethiek? in: Ethiek als Waagstuk, 1969, 43–45.

[66] Cf. the attempts to deduce the hypostasation of wisdom from Persian and Egyptian mythology in Rankin, O. S., Israel's Wisdom Literature, 1936, 225ff. Cf. also Lang, B., Frau Weisheit, 1975, 147ff., for a brief look at the different opinions about the personified wisdom and his own contribution (the wisdom is the personified »Schulweisheit als Lehrerin«) to the debate.

[67] Cf. Gese, H. op. cit. 72f.

There are two commonly accepted ways in which this knowledge could be interpreted: One is to explain this knowledge as purely secular and the other is to accept a natural theology in the sense that the acquired knowledge of the created order provides sufficient knowledge of the creator of this order.

These possibilities don't apply for the wisdom literature of Israel. This can be proven by concentrating on the concept *yir'at Jahweh* in Israel's wisdom literature.

J. Becker has provided us with a detailed study[68] of the concept »fear of the Lord« in the Old Testament. He demonstrates how originally fear was the spontaneous reaction of man before the deity and that only later it developed into a cultic and ethical concept. This semantical transition allows for an interpretation of the concept in the Old Testament as obedience towards God and as obedience towards the law[69]. Within the Elohistic documents the concept of the »fear of the Lord« normally implies obedience towards God[70]. In Deuteronomy and documents under Deuteronomistic influence (e.g. Neh. and Jer.) the cultic aspect is dominant, especially as loyalty of the covenant community[71].

The contrasting ethical content of the concept as piety is, according to Becker, the result of the wisdom tradition[72]. McKane also maintains that the »fear of the Lord« was only later combined with wisdom in the shift from education to piety[73]. This tradition eventually results in the religious ands ethical content of the concept with Jesus Sirach — so much so that the basic theme of Sirach can be characterised in terms of it[74]. The ethical content is, however, more and more interpreted in a legalistic manner[75], which is naturally related to the tradition in which the wisdom and the law began to operate on the same level. In Haspeckers' study the obedience of

---

[68] Becker, J., Gottesfurcht im Alten Testament, 1966. Cf. also Nissen, A., Gott und der Nächste im antiken Judentum, 1974, 183; and Oosterhoff, B. J., De Vreze des Heren in het Oude Testament, 1949.

[69] Cf. Becker, J. op. cit. 55 and 84.

[70] Cf. Wolff, H. W., EvTh 29 (1969), 62 f.

[71] Becker, J. op. cit. 123–183 and Oosterhoff, B. J. op. cit. 18 ff. Deist, F., Die Betekenissfeer van die Leksikale Morfeem y-r-' in die Profetiese Boeke van die Ou Testament, 1978, 107–108 and 125–126, maintains the concept *yr'* as designation of the relation of obedience between Jahweh and his people. The origin of such a designation is then related to the Ancient Near Eastern Law (vasal treaties).

[72] Ibid. 210–261.

[73] McKane, W. op. cit. 368. Whybray, R. N. op. cit. 96–98 even goes further and postulates that the »fear of Jahweh« is secondarily attached to the teaching of wisdom and almost become the designation of the syllabus of the wisdom school!

[74] Cf. Haspecker, J., Gottesfurcht bei Jesus Sirach, 1967, 87. 198 and 201.

[75] Cf. Becker, J. op. cit. 262–282 and Fuz, W. op. cit. 293.

the law as content of the *yir'at Jahweh*, is balanced by the real piety of the personal relation towards God: In Jesus Sirach the »fear of the Lord« is represented as »Frömmigkeit die die Spannung von Gottverbundenheit und Unterwerfung unter Gott, von bewußter Bejahung der Majestät Gottes und seiner Menschenfreundlichkeit voll aufnimmt und aushält und zu einer harmonischen Einheit zusammenfügt, ohne das eine auf Kosten des anderen zu verkürzen«[76].

It may be accepted that the cultic connotation of the *yir'at Jahweh* is more fundamental or original than is the ethical connotation, but it is hard to believe that a process of evolution takes place in such a way that the ethical connotation is substituted for the cultic connotation. The worship of God is not a cultically limited activity, but expresses the all-embracing relation of man towards God. The ethical connotation in other words, is complementary to the cultic connotation. The cultic and the ethical elements are equivalent aspects of the order provided by God and He instructs man to honour both. We wholeheartedly agree with A. Nissen's clarifying description: »In dieser Offenbarungsordnung ist daher »Furcht Gottes« dasjenige sich als Unterwerfung unter Gott vollziehende Verhalten, in dem das rechte Tun gegenüber Gott und dasjenige gegenüber dem Nächsten geeint sind als die beiden zusammenhängenden Aspekte derselben Forderung, Gott als den allein Setzenden und Verfügenden gemäß seiner Ordnung im Lebensvollzug anzuerkennen: Furcht Gottes ist als Gottesverehrung die Einheit von Kultus und Ethos und ist dies so, daß der eine Aspekt nur mit dem anderen und durch den anderen hindurch in der gottgeordneten Weise wirklich ist.«[77]

The concept of the *yir'at Jahweh* in Proverbs definitely includes the ethical aspect as demonstrated in Prov 8 13 14 16 22 4 23 17—18 and 29 25. In all these verses accent is laid on the *yir'at Jahweh* as a quality of the pious man — a quality which keeps him from evil (8 13 14 16), brings about modesty (22 4) and ensures a future (23 17—18).

The *yir'at Jahweh* is not the ethical aspect of human existence in its active obedience and trust in the absolute authority of God[78] nor an expression of modesty as the ethics of wisdom[79]. The *yir'at Jahweh* in the Proverbs is not represented »als bloßes Mittel der Lebenssicherung«[80], but as much more comprehensive. This is made explicit through the designation of the *yir'at Jahweh* as the *rē'šit* (Prov 1 7), the *tĕhillâ* (Prov 9 10) and the *mûsār* (Prov 15 33) of wisdom[81]. These concepts do not signify that the

---

[76] Haspecker, J. op. cit. 338.
[77] Nissen, A. op. cit. 183—184.
[78] Cf. Kayatz, C. B., Einführung in die alttestamentliche Weisheit, 1969, 33.
[79] Preuss, H. D., EvTh 30 (1970), 399.
[80] Correctly evaluated by Hempel, J., Das Ethos des Alten Testaments, 1938, 25.
[81] Compare also Job 28 28 Ps 111 10 and Sir 1 14.

yir'at Jahweh is the main constituent of wisdom or the sum-total of wisdom, but rather that the *yir'at Jahweh* leads to wisdom. The *yir'at Jahweh*, in other words, is the scope or sphere in which wisdom is possible and conceivable[82]. Within the framework of the *yir'at Jahweh*, wisdom is realised. Wisdom as the cognitive ability to recognise the created order and
• the ethos which it demands, is only possible within the *yir'at Jahweh*. The *yir'at Jahweh* is not a gift of wisdom, but precedes wisdom. The *yir'at Jahweh* is accordingly used as an object in Prov 23 17–18: The reality of the *yir'at Jahweh*, in direct opposition to that of the sinners, must be envied (cf. also Prov 3 7). The recognition of the principle of the *yir'at Jahweh*, brings about real wisdom. We can therefore translate the *yir'at Jahweh* with religion[83]. U. Skladny describes it as follows: »Jahwe-Furcht ist die gefühls- und bewußtseinmäßige Anerkennung des Totalitätsanspruches Gottes, die sich in religiösen und sittlichen Handeln äußert.«[84] It is not an aspect of ethical behaviour, but the premise and condition which constitutes ethical conduct. The *yir'at Jahweh* is the premise for real existence in *ṣĕdāqâ*. The decision in confrontation with the *yir'at Jahweh* (religion) is therefore a decision for life or death (cf. Prov 9 10–11 and Prov 23 17–18)[85].

The *yir'at Jahweh* of Proverbs usually evaluated as the religious and ethical aspect of human conduct[86], now becomes the very manner of religious existence: In other words, it becomes the overriding existential[87]. It is the mode of real existence.

It might be objected that wisdom as a gift of God[88] (cf. Ex 28 3 31 3.6 35 31.35 36 1f. I Kings 3 4 5 9 Ps 51 8 119 98 Job 28.35 11 Prov 2 6 8 22 Qoh 2 26 Dan 1 17 and 2 21.23) and the concept of the *yir'at Jahweh* in the wisdom literature occur relatively late in the Israelite traditions and are under influence of a process of theological re-interpretation. I do not deny that theological re-interpretation took place: indeed, one can point out that the structural position of sayings such as Prov 1 7 9 10 and 23 17 are later insertions into these contexts. That, however, does not make the older wisdom non-religious[89]. This tradition of theological re-interpretation does

---

[82] Thus, the concept includes even more than just the »beginning« of wisdom, cf. Oosterhoff, B. J. op. cit. 85 f.

[83] Cf. Procksch, O., Theologie des Alten Testaments, 1950, 610–614; Gese, H. op. cit. 178–179, and Pfeiffer, R. H., IEJ 5 (1955), 41–48.

[84] Skladny, U. op. cit. 15. Cf. also Oosterhoff, B. J. op. cit. 87 and 134.

[85] Cf. our discussion of Prov 23 17–18 in par. 3.1.3.

[86] Cf. Würthwein, E., Die Weisheit Ägyptens und das Alte Testament, 1959, 4.

[87] Against Preuss, H. D. op. cit. 399 who interprets the *yir'at Jahweh* as »Ausdruck weisheitlicher Demut.«

[88] Noth, M., VTS 3, 1955, 225 ff.; Crenshaw, J. L. op. cit. 228 f. and McKane, W. op. cit. 368.

[89] It is sufficiently demonstrated by von Rad, G. op.cit. 97 ff.

not reduce the older wisdom to speculative reflection, but provides the essential frame of interpretation. Right from the beginning, wisdom shows no discrepancy between social ethics and religion.

It is meaningful that the theological interpretation of wisdom as a gift of God and possible within the *yir'at Jahweh* is made explicit in the wisdom. This theological achievement cuts any suggestion of natural theology off at the roots. Within the framework of the *yir'at Jahweh* the two poles of the truth meet in harmony: wisdom and revelation (or reason (philosophy) and revelation). It is wisdom in search of understanding that penetrates everything created, becomes acquainted with it and sees God as the Creator of it all. The knowledge of the created order, becomes revealed knowledge. This knowledge through which the unity of reality is made comprehensible, is impossible without belief — without the *yir'at Jahweh*. Knowledge of the created order does not contradict the will of God, because the God who reveals himself is the God who created the universe. Within the *yir'at Jahweh* wisdom finds its limits and its goal!

Later we will see that this knowledge contains an ethos (explicit in the admonition) of coherence between »orderly« existence and knowledge of God: An ethos not of conduct and rule, but of modesty (to submit oneself to the majesty of God) and wise reflection (cf. Prov 1 22 10 11 10 14 11 11 11 12 12 9 13 3 17 27, etc.).

4.5   The Ethos of the Wisdom

In the preceding paragraphs different aspects of the ethos of wisdom are already manifest: the importance of the admonition, the authority of wisdom, the kind of knowledge provided in the instructions of wisdom, wisdom's relation to the law and wisdom's boundary and goal within the framework of the *yir'at Jahweh*.

A major problem, however, exists: Where is wisdom to be placed in the context of Old Testament revelation[90]? One gets the impression that this problem is mainly due to the lack of a sound qualification of the knowledge expressed in the wisdom teaching and the kind of ethos deducable from it. In the course of this chapter an attempt will be made to evaluate the wisdom as a necessary element of Old Testament theology to illuminate its ethos. To achieve this goal one has to consider the wisdom as one entire tradition, because as a tradition it provides perspective on the theological interpretation.

---

[90] Cf. the problems put forward by Hasel, G. F., ZAW 86 (1974), 68f.; Priest, J. F., JBR 31 (1963), 275–282; Toombs, L. E., JBR 22 (1955), 193–196; Lêvêque, L., Le contrepoint theologique apporté par la reflexion sapientielle, in: Questions Disputees d'Ancient Testament, (ed. Brekelmans C.), 1974, 183–202, and Murphy, R. E., CBQ 29 (1967), 407–418.

It is impossible to maintain the wisdom teachings as theological ethics without according them a place within the Old Testament history of revelation[91], because the theological context of the wisdom is a premise for the correct evaluation of the ethos proclaimed in it. L. E. Toombs[92] correctly lays emphasis on the revelation of God in which the wisdom must have its place, because wisdom transcends theological morality.

Various attempts have been made to justify the wisdom as an essential aspect of Old Testament theology. H-J. Kraus in his study of Prov 8 22ff.[93] provides perspective for the interpretation of Prov 8 22ff., but accordingly also for that of wisdom as a whole. He points out that the wisdom has in fact a place within the acts of revelation of God and mainly in its anticipation of the New Testament. In the wisdom man finds the subjective realisation of Gods will of salvation (Heilswillen)[94].

Occasionally the Old Testament covenant is maintained as the theological context of wisdom[95]. E. Würthwein stresses the importance of the covenant-people throughout the Old Testament and that the prohibitions and exhortations must be viewed accordingly, but in the end he distinguishes sharply between the God of the covenant and the God of the wisdom. The God of the wisdom is a retributional God[96]. In the end he accepts the principle of a created order of God to which wisdom is oriented. Within this context the dogma of retribution is the dominant one, according to Würthwein.

Hubbard postulates various points of historical contact between the wisdom literature and the covenant conception in order to maintain that wisdom literature is covenant literature[97]. Wisdom indeed plays a prominent role during the period of the Israelite monarchy and the prophets are influenced by the wisdom movement and by wisdom concepts, but that does not necessarily provide enough reason to maintain the covenant as the theological context of wisdom.

E. Beaucamp also attempts to demonstrate how the Sinai covenant is the characteristic feature in the wisdom literature, despite the fact that wisdom as such is an international phenomenon of the Ancient Near East. Israel is influenced by the aristocratic wisdom (from Egypt), but in Israel it went

---

[91] Put forward by Schmid, H. H. op. cit. 201.
[92] JBR 23 (1955), 193–196.
[93] Kraus, H-J., Die Verkündigung der Weisheit, 1951.
[94] Ibid. 26ff.
[95] Weinfeld, M., VT 23 (1973), 64ff.; Würthwein, E., Die Weisheit Ägyptens und das Alte Testament, 1959, 8ff.; Hubbard, D. A., The Wisdom Movement and Israel's Covenant Faith, Tyndale Bulletin 17 (1966), 3–33; Beaucamp, E., Man's Destiny in the Book of Wisdom, 1970, 28ff., and van Oyen, H., Ethik des Alten Testaments, 1967, 89ff.
[96] Ibid. 7–9.
[97] Hubbard, D. A. op. cit. 3–33.

through the refinery of the Sinai covenant: »In Israel Wisdom is presented always as a free gift, as the individual makes the same response to her as did the people as a whole to the divine Covenant at Sinai.«[98]

The peculiarity of each culture (correctly understood by Beaucamp) must be maintained, but Becaucamp does not successfully demonstrate a relation between wisdom and the covenant nor how the covenant is the context of interpretation. It seem as if his solution is drawn from a supposed analogy between law stipulations and wisdom sayings. Lack of factual data in his study makes it difficult for one to be convinced of the assumption that the wisdom forms the »door« to the covenant[99].

J. Goldingay is sceptical about any attempt to determine the context of Biblical Theology from a wisdom perspective. The content of wisdom is simply what redemptive history calls keeping the covenant[100]. According to Goldingay, the redemptive aspect so dominant in the so-called »Heilsgeschichte«, cannot be ignored in the wisdom literature. In the final analysis redemptive history becomes the dominant principle in biblical theology for Goldingay and the wisdom literature is nothing but an illustration and explication of one aspect of that principle[101].

Irrespective of the positive ideas advanced by Goldingay, two problems remain: a reluctance to develop an understanding of wisdom from the tradition of wisdom in Israel itself and a very broad connotation of redemptive history, which includes almost every aspect of the different traditions of the Old Testament. Such an ill-founded generalisation well-nigh precludes lucid thinking concerning the content of Biblical Theology.

A very popular approach is to determine the context of the wisdom from the experience of reality (Wirklichkeitsverständnis) by the people of the Ancient Near East. Major exponents of this approach are G. von Rad[102] and H. Gese[103] while others have followed in their footsteps. The world is experienced as order: Wisdom is God's order of this world. In this respect the wisdom becomes comparable to the Egyptian *MAAT*[104].

---

[98] Beaucamp, E. op. cit. 28 and 40.

[99] Ibid. 27 ff. Cf. also the criticism of Formen, C., Hibbert Journal 60 (1962), 129 f., and Baumgärtel, F., Eigenart der alttestamentlichen Frömmigkeit, 1931, 32.

[100] Goldingay, J., The Evangelical Quarterly 51 (1979), 203.

[101] Ibid. 204–206.

[102] Cf. von Rad, G., Weisheit in Israel, 100 f. and 189 ff.

[103] Gese, H., Lehre und Wirklichkeit in der alten Weisheit, 1958, 36 f. and 43 f.

[104] Cf. Brunner, H., Die Weisheitliteratur, Ägyptologie, Handbuch der Orientalistik, I/2 1952, 93 ff.; VT 8 (1958), 426–428, and Whybray, R. N. op. cit. 54 f. Cf. also Ringgren, H., Word and Wisdom, 1947, 49 ff.; Schmid, H. H. op. cit. 159 ff., and Perdue, L. G., Wisdom and Cult, 1977, 19–28 and 135–137.

This conception of order is closely linked with God's act of creation. So the accent shifts from the aspect of order to Jahweh as Creator[105]. The God who created the world is then the central theme of the wisdom. Wisdom is then assigned a place in what we can call a theology of creation[106].

Often the concept of order is absolutised to mean causal inevitability: human conduct is bound hand and foot to the rigid causality of act-consequence. God who maintains this order also retributes man according to his good or evil act. Hence the dogma of retribution is considered the basic theme in the wisdom[107]. The »schicksalwirkende Tatsphäre«[108] should consequently be the guiding dogma of wisdom's ethics.

For the deduction of ethical assumptions from the wisdom teachings it may be well to keep the element of retribution in mind, but it does not as such provide a theological context for the wisdom.

The most extreme view critical of wisdom is expressed by H. D. Preuss in two of his papers[109]. Preuss does maintain the concept of the world as order, but more accent is laid on the act-consequence- (behaviour-reward)-relation as the constitutive element. This fatalistic philosophy rules the empire of the older wisdom according to Preuss. The dogma of retribution is the exclusive dogma in the older wisdom, as can be seen in the reaction of Job and Qohelet against it. This crisis within wisdom itself is not accidental, but typical of the very nature of wisdom (1970, 400 ff.).

Preuss considers it impossible to incorporate the wisdom within the frame of Old Testament revelation (1970, 412). The presumption that the wisdom for its theological context depends on the covenant or on a theology of creation, is also rejected by Preuss (1970, 414 f.). Preuss also disapproves of C. Westermann's attempts to accommodate the wisdom

---

[105] Cf. Priest, J. F. op. cit. 281–282; Stecher, R., ZKTh 30 (1953), 424; Rankin, O. S., Israel's Wisdom Literature, 1936, 9 ff., and Hulsbosch, A., Sagesse creatrice et éducatrice, Augustinianum II (1962), 16 ff.

[106] Cf. Zimmerli, W. op. cit. 188 ff. and also his Grundriß der alttestamentlichen Theologie, 1975, 138 f.

[107] Cf. Fichtner, J. op. cit. 25. 62 ff. and 124; Skladny, U. op. cit. 71 ff. and 89 f.; Würthwein, E. op. cit. 9, and Loader, J. A., OTWSA 15–16, 1972–1973, 43–48. Rankin, O. S., Israel's Wisdom Literature, 1936, 78 ff., points out that the Deuteronomistic theory of reward is reflected in Proverbs as a rigid dogma.

[108] Cf. Lang, B. op. cit. 101. This concept is taken over by Lang from Koch, K., ZThK 52 (1955), 1–42, who objected against the juridical connotation of »retribution« and coined the concept of a »schicksalwirkende Tatsphäre« (32) as a useful alternative. A new approach to the problem is made by Keller, C.-A., Zum sogenannten Vergeltungsglauben im Proverbienbuch, in: FS Zimmerli, 1977, 223–238, when he attempts to solve the problem with the sociological principle of »Leistung« and »Gegenleistung«.

[109] Preuss, H. D., EvTh 30 (1970), 393–417, and Questions Disputes d'Ancient Testament (ed. Brekelmans, C.), 1974, 165–181.

within the »Segenshandeln Jahwes«[110]. The blessing of Jahweh is seldom referred to in the Book of Proverbs (3 33 and 10 22). In the rest of the Old Testament the blessing of Jahweh cannot be isolated from the historical and eschatological aspects which are irreconcilable with the wisdom (1970, 414).

Preuss does not ignore the wisdom influence on the other traditions such as the history of salvation, the Prophets, the Law and the Psalms, but here the »Jahwismus« acts as a catalyst so that a major crisis like that of the wisdom tradition itself is here avoided. Every aspect of the Old Testament wisdom can be illustrated with analogies or parallels from non-biblical wisdom literature. The wisdom is an international phenomenon and as such a »Fremdkörper« in Israel and proclaims »nichts spezifisch Jahwistisches« (1974, 173). The following quotation illustrates the extremity to which Preuss is ready to go: »Die Weisheit redet nicht von Erzvätern, Bund, Verheißung und Erfüllung, Mose, Auszug, Gottesrecht, Israel als Bundesvolk, nicht von David und Davidsbund, nicht von Geschichte und Eschatologie, und sie steht damit außerhalb des für das Alte Testament Spezifischen.«[111] Wisdom is then a non-Israelite tradition which stands in an unbridgeable conflict with belief in Jahweh. In the context of Old Testament revelation wisdom is shunted onto the siding of no contribution. People who try to place wisdom as part of the Old Testament do so because they *ex officio* understand their task within that framework[112].

Certain objections can be raised against the views of A. D. Preuss: His attempt to characterise the kind of knowledge proclaimed in the wisdom, is insufficient. The logical reduction of the concept of order to a rigid dogma of act-consequence constitutes a travesty of the real state of affairs. He takes no account of what others have called optimism in the wisdom. Is there any truth to this optimism? Or are optimism and pessimism the absolute consequences of the act-consequence dogma? Preuss merely maintains the act-consequence dogma as a non-Jahwistic feature and finds his »proof« in the diametrically opposite positions of Job and Qohelet. He does not, however, give account of the fact that the dogma in question is not totally nullified and voided in Job and Qohelet. The supplementary aspects of Job and Qohelet are not considered.

It is evident that on the horizon of Preuss' argument appears the silhouette of the dualism: a dualism between religion and social ethics (between religion and world experience!)[113]. For that reason wisdom represents nothing typically Jahwistic and therefore it must be in absolute conflict with Jahwism. Knowledge and belief are polarised by Preuss. An

---

[110] Westermann, C., Das Alte Testament und Jesus Christus, 1968, 46ff.
[111] Loc. cit. 414.
[112] Loc.cit. (1974) 177.
[113] Cf. von Rad, G. op.cit. 87.

artificial gulf is created between the literature influenced by the wisdom, but nevertheless harmonised by the Jahwistic belief, and the wisdom literature as such. Non-biblical analogies and parallels can be provided with regard to the wisdom literature as such, and therefore it must be non-Jahwistic. If the wisdom was such a »Fremdkörper« in Israel, how then is it possible that the major traditions of the Old Testament are brought into contact with the wisdom and are even identified with wisdom[114]? Could an identification take place within wisdom if it were totally non-Jahwistic? The theological milieu elaborated in the tradition of wisdom itself, testifies to the fact that the wisdom was not such a »Fremdkörper«, but instead brought about a necessary renewal in the history of revelation. That does not mean that the wisdom become totally estranged from its original ancient Near Eastern setting, revealing none of its traces, but it has its proper place within the Israelite religion and reveals characteristics peculiar to Israelite culture.

The wisdom is not a matter of *ex officio* religious treatment, but an irreplaceable element of Old Testament Theology! To illustrate the impact of wisdom and its place in Old Testament Theology we must recap briefly what has already been discovered concerning the knowledge proclaimed in the wisdom and what kind of ethos is intrinsic to it.

We have established that the very nature of the admonition, together with its motivation, mediates reasonable knowledge[115]: Knowledge about created plants, birds, human beings and other cosmic features. These things do not exist chaotically, but are determined by a divine order. The purposive activity of wise thought in attempting to grasp this created order, to recognise and to designate the antithesis of this order, results in the knowledge of the creator of this order. Knowledge then becomes revealed knowledge, because it points to the knowledge (wisdom) of God through which He determines the order. It does not, however, develop into a natural theology, because the knowledge of the created order as knowledge of God in Israel is only possible within the framework of the *yir'at Jahweh*. With the recognition of this premise, knowledge and revelation are harmonized: belief and reason form a synthesis. This is the main reason why it is possible that the wisdom available to man, is the Wisdom which transcendently exists with God (cf. Prov 8 22ff. Job 28 and Sir 24).

The knowledge (wisdom), as described above, cannot therefore be that of speculative world experience or secular science, but it inherently implies an ethos − a responsibility towards one's own ethical conduct.

The ultimate goal of the education of wisdom, of the knowledge provided, is to meet the requirements of an ethical existence (cf. Prov 22 6). To the man of discretion, wisdom guards his own conduct (cf. Prov 14 8).

---

[114] Cf. par. 4.3.
[115] Cf. par. 4.1.ff.

The instruction of wisdom intends to make one a competent being — wise in conduct (Prov 19 20).

W. Zimmerli[116], therefore, correctly points out the central position of *listen* in the wisdom instructions, but to listen is not an educational goal in itself. The instruction to listen to wisdom is so prominent, because it provides knowledge of the ethos to be followed. That is why wisdom is an instruction against the loose-living woman (Prov 5 3ff. and 7 1ff.). Acceptance of the invitation of Mrs. Wisdom, is the acceptance of a new way of living and does not imply exclusively the acquisition of cognitive knowledge (Prov 9 6). The acceptance of wisdom has ethical consequences (cf. Prov 3 13f. 3 16 3 22f. 4 22 and 13 14).

An interesting distinction is made in Prov 19 25 in this respect: The uneducated (*petî*) learns by means of the example — he must be shown how to live, but the *nābōn* is capable of harmonizing knowledge and reality — of reconciling knowledge and ethos. The ethical instruction can be forced (so to speak) on the uneducated, but the real understanding of the ethos as the complement of knowledge is possible only for the wise man. The synthesis of both is accomplished in the sage who knows that his knowledge of the created order is not in the order of factual knowledge, but is made possible in the personal relation towards God. The wisdom is not a substitute for the personal relation, but wisdom accomplishes the relation because it contains the ethos which prescribes and constitutes the only meaningful relation.

Might this be the reason why wisdom is personified? In the personfied wisdom the personal relation can be constituted. According to the Sinai tradition and the prophets the revelation occurs in the personal relation of Jahweh and the individual. The wisdom personified (hypostatised) makes it possible to represent the relation of man towards wisdom as a personal relationship.

The immanent ethos of the wisdom is often made explicit in the admonition (as pointed out earlier in par. 4.1). When man is confrontated by and knows the created order, he is not only obliged to recognize this order, but more importantly, to realise this order in his own conduct. Violation of this order on the part of man, does not abolish the order of Jahweh, but rather makes the chaos a reality in his own conduct with far-reaching consequences[117]. The accomplishment of the ethos consists in the act of personal subordination to wisdom, and therefore to the created order. Obedience to wisdom implies subordination to the created order. The admonition requires the ethos of an existence devoted to and in harmony with the order of creation.

---

[116] Zimmerli, W. op. cit. 181. »Listening« is according to Zimmerli the authoritative (school) invitation of wisdom because the essence of wisdom is *leqaḥ*.

[117] Cf. Kaiser, O., NZSThR 14 (1972), 21.

In this sense the ethos of wisdom is not based on proclaimed laws, but on the created order which in no way directly conflicts with reason. Let us put it positively: Because the created order is comprehensible it can be the foundation and goal of an ethos. The ethos of the wisdom is characterized by the tension between knowing the order and having to realize it. The two are not in paradox, but the order as demanded order implies a tension, because what is demanded, is yet the unrealised order. There is neither a conflict between belief and reason, nor between belief and ethics[118]. The ideal theological synthesis is the accomplishment of both. A thoroughly anthropocentric ethos in the wisdom, is therefore impossible[119].

In a secondary sense we might say that even in the wisdom an ethos is proclaimed which demands subordination to the will of God[120], because the will of God (in the *tôrâ*) is not in contradiction to God's created order (cf. our discussion on *tôrâ* and wisdom). But, we would prefer to maintain the ethos of the wisdom as based on the created order. In the *logos* of creation wisdom's ethos found its setting. The ethical order therefore cannot be in opposition to the created order[121]. The wise man has the ability to trace (so to speak) the revealed order of creation and to find the norm of conduct accordingly. This ethos demands a reestablishment of a new order – an order of personal, social and of world experience. It is possible only through the knowledge represented in wisdom and through faith in Jahweh (Prov 21 30).

According to Zimmerli there can be no question of a presumed order or a »schöpfungsmäßigen Gebundenheit«[122] of man to found the ethos of wisdom. The ethos focuses on the benefit of the individual (*tôb lĕʾādām*). For the free and self-determined being the first priority is not to determine one's duty, but to realise one's possibilities[123]. Real piety then consists of being endlessly on guard to protect one's existence in this world. Such an anthropocentric and utilitarian[124] ethos is foreign to the wisdom. The real unity of ethos and belief is broken up into a neo-Kantean dualism[125]. When the unity of ethos and belief (revealed knowledge) is jeopardized, an inevitable dualism or the ethicization of every aspect of religion results[126].

---

[118] Hempel, J., Das Ethos des Alten Testaments, 1938, 25 ff.

[119] Lindblom, J., Wisdom in the Old Testament Prophets, VTS 3, 1955, 197.

[120] Cf. Burrows, M., in: Essays in Old Testament Ethics (ed. Crenshaw, J. L.) 1974, 228.

[121] Cf. Schmid, H. H. op.cit. 19–21 and 105 ff. Cf. also von Rad, G. op.cit. 122 ff.

[122] Zimmerli, W. op. cit. 192.

[123] Ibid. 194.

[124] Cf. also Baumgärtel, F. op.cit. 38.

[125] The struggle to overcome this dualism is also to be seen in the study of Fuss, W. op.cit. 311 ff. who attempts to reconcile a theological ethos and the wisdom ethos in Sirach.

[126] Such a logical ethicization is to be found in the study of Ricoeur, P., The Symbolism of Evil, 1969, 314 f. God then becomes the solely ethical God and the law the bond between man and God. Law and Covenant then result in an ethical determination.

Order-oriented thinking is the pulse of wisdom. The general introduction of Prov 1 1–7[127] already makes it clear. The final clause in v. 3 introduces three concepts (*ṣedɛq*, *mišpāṭ* and *mêšārîm*) which are of immense importance and very difficult to explain without a concept of order. These concepts are not synonyms, each of them bearing its own specific connotation, but there must be a logical bond between them allowing them to function co-ordinately, not to the exclusion of each other. It occurs that the *ṣedɛq*[128] represents the ideal order — the order of existence. It is the *ṣaddîq* who lives in harmony with this order. The realization of the *ṣedɛq* means to live according to the real order[129]. It is the order of existence. The divine order penetrates social and individual existence[130]. It is therefore intelligible that the instruction of wisdom is *ṣedɛq* (Prov 8 8. Cf. also 12 17). The king as guarantee of this order, can proclaim the *ṣedɛq* (cf. prov 8 16 and 25 5). It is his duty to ensure that the *ṣedɛq* is maintained and that it is possible for each of his citizens (especially the under-privileged) to materialise the *ṣedɛq* (cf. Prov 31 9).

mišpāṭ is most probably to be understood as the action or activity (mainly juridical) which materialises the *ṣedɛq*. The *mišpāṭ* is the juridical explication of the *ṣedɛq* and Jahweh himself is the patron of the *'orḥôt mišpāṭ*[131] (Prov 2 8), or the king too, as his representative (Prov 24 23 and 29 4). It is the testimony of the bad witness which violates the *mišpāṭ* (Prov 19 28); the wicked one resists the *mišpāṭ* (Prov 21 7) and does not know what it means (28 5), but it is the pleasure of the *ṣaddîq* (Prov 21 15) and more pleasing to Jahweh than sacrifice (Prov 21 3). Thus, it is evident that the *mišpāṭ* means the act by which the *ṣedɛq* is realised and that it is the wicked and crooked men who violate this order. In the final analysis, God is the patron of the *mišpāṭ* and the act which constitutes *mišpāṭ* is from Jahweh (Prov 16 11).

The *mêšārîm*[132] finally would be the inner or personal righteousness. It means the individual and ethical realization of the *ṣedɛq* (Prov 8 6 and 23 16).

---

[127] Cf. Prov 2 9.

[128] The interpretation is restricted to the occurrences of *ṣedɛq* in Proverbs.

[129] Cf. Schmid, H. H., Gerechtigkeit als Weltordnung, 1968, 96—98, 157—160.

[130] Cf. Bühlmann, W., Vom rechten Reden und Schweigen, 1976, 99. According to Bühlmann (99 and 167) the expression *šiptê ṣedɛq* must be translated with »ordnungsgemäßen Reden«, which supports the order connotation of *ṣedɛq*.

[131] The expression is used in a juridical sense, cf. 8 20 and 17 23. Cf. also *mišpāṭ* in a juridical sense, Prov 17 23 19 28 18 5 and 16 33.

[132] Olivier, J. P. J., The Old Babylonian Mešarum-Edict and the Old Testament, 1978, 317, makes evident that the *mêšārîm* is a universal norm which coincides with the created order. It was also the main purpose of the *mešarum*-edict in Babylon to create and restore order in the socio-economic life (143ff.). In the Old Testament the concept later became an ethical term and likewise a characteristic virtue of the God-fearing and the wise (319ff.). Cf. also Schmid, H. H. op. cit. 9ff.

We are therefore inclined to maintain the concept of order as a basic premise in the discipline (Prov 1 3a) of wisdom: An order of existence given by God requiring materialization, both officially and individually.

Any action against this order entails its violation and in the end leads to self-destruction (Prov 1 10–19 and Prov 4 13–19)[133]. The acceptance is the realisation of the order. But we must always remember that the recognition of the order of existence is the recognition of the world-order or the created order. It is therefore not surprising that the creative activity of God is explicated (Prov 3 19ff.) directly following the discussion of the religious character of wisdom (Prov 3 1–18. Cf. also Prov 8 22f. Job 28 Sir 24 and Ps 104 24f.).

H-J. Hermisson acknowledges the importance of order-oriented thinking in the wisdom, but he also claims to find some wisdom sayings which do not reflect this idea[134]. Such a proverb is Prov 25 23:

> The rain is born of the north wind,
> the ravaged face of a backbiting tongue. (JB)

This proverb does not deny world order. In fact, this proverb gives substance to the concept of order and is in accordance with the traditional act-consequence dogma. The unity of world-experience is stressed in the sense that the cosmic order does not exclude the human (existence) order. In view of the cosmic regularity, the northwind brings rain, another ultimate regularity runs parallel with it: a backbiting tongue brings about strife and quarrel. The bad consequence of malicious gossip is almost as inevitable as are consequences in nature. The observance of strict order in various spheres makes it possible to see analogies between phenomena which logically do not operate in the same sphere[135]. The so-called »Wertsystem«[136] of good and bad is not in opposition to order-oriented thinking, but an aspect of its logical realization. Judging the consequence of an act as bad or good, already comprises a system of order priorities.

At this point we may conclude that the knowledge of wisdom is not in contraditction with revelation. It is knowledge of the created order. Wisdom, however, is not purely cognitive knowledge, but implies an ethos: an ethos demanding an orderly existence — a re-creation of order in view of

---

[133] The same lesson is taught with the predication of the zārâ (Prov 2 16f. 5 and 7) as an examplification of the wicked and evil as such.

[134] Hermisson, H-J. op. cit. 140ff.

[135] A similar approach would show that the concept of order cannot be excluded from Prov 10 5 10 18b and 12 1b as Hermisson, H.-J. op. cit. 154 maintains.

[136] Ibid. 154. It is noteworthy that Hermisson sometimes excludes only the second stichos of a proverb (cf. eg. 10 18b and 12 1b) which manifests the system of values. The aspect of comparison, so dominant in the wisdom sayings, and its role in constituting the truth of a saying, is thus ignored.

the recognition of the created order. Wisdom, thus, is the norm according to which ethical conduct is directed, the norm according to which meaningful existence is oriented[137]!

The tension of wisdom's ethos consists not so much in the paradox between being chosen by God as grace (gift) and the required sanctification of his name[138], but rather between knowledge and ethics. The *imago Dei* (Nachahmung Gottes)[139] is according to M. Buber »ein zum Bilde Gottes hin Geschaffen-Sein«[140]. The *imago Dei* can only be attached to the ethos of the wisdom secondarily. In as far as the human act reaffirms order in view of one's knowledge of this order, the aspect of the *imago Dei* is realized.

Knowledge of God and his created order is inherently the act of righteousness. This ethos is explicitly demanded in the admonitions. The admonition by nature is not simply threatening, but intends and illuminates the act of reaffirming order. Hence, the law is not an enumeration of taboos with threats to forestall ill-behaviour and self-defilement; its main intention is the re-establishing of order.

The ethos of wisdom is not a rigid system of morality or a form of legalism. It is the religious existential — it is the way of living in harmony with the knowledge of the created order and therefore in harmony with the order of God. Without the knowledge and understanding it would have been an abstract system of morality.

The realization of the ethos of wisdom means prosperity and real life (Prov 3 21–26) — it is the realization of the *šālôm*[141] because it is by wisdom that life and *šālôm* are created (Prov 3 2 3 17). The *šālôm* is the quality of an existence in harmony with God (Prov 3 17) and God himself makes it possible (cf. Is 26 12 45 7 52 7 57 19 60 17 Hag 2 9 and Ps 122 7). The *šālôm* is the reality contrasting with that of evil and wicked men (Prov 12 20 Ps 34 15 35 20 85 9 Is 48 22 57 21 and 59 8). Human conduct in righteousness explicates the *šālôm* (Is 32 17 and 57 2).

The experience and knowledge of order as created order, does not imply that man has the order at his disposal and under his control[142]. Wisdom's reflection is directed towards the order and rules which can be experienced in wisdom's environment, and knows itself incompetent to lay down rules for God's activity, because God, in the final analysis, is free in

---

[137] Cf. Pfeiffer, R. op. cit. 107 ff.

[138] Van Oyen, H., Ethik des Alten Testaments, 1967, 43.

[139] Ibid. 49.

[140] Quoted by van Oyen, H. op. cit. 45.

[141] Cf. van Oyen, H. op. cit. 58; Gese, H. op. cit. 57, and Schmid, H. H., Salôm: »Frieden« im Alten Orient und im Alten Testament, 1971, especially 53 ff.

[142] Cf. Gese, H. op. cit. (1958) 58; Rendtorff, R., Geschichtliches und weisheitliches Denken im Alten Testament, in: FS. W. Zimmerli, 1977, 349, and von Rad, G. op. cit. 136 f.

his acts. It is the order created by God which remains at His disposal (Prov
10 3 14 21 14 31 16 2 17 5 19 17 20 9 21 13 22 2 and 27 1). Recognition of the
order as God's order gives substance to the most peculiar characteristic of
the ethos of wisdom, namely that it does not proclaim an ethos of conduct
and rule, but that of modesty, humility and wise reflection (Prov 10 11 10 14
11 11.12 12 9 13 3 17 27, etc.). In this respect it is intelligible that such a
premium is placed on the correct choice and sober use of one's words and
on reticence as an attitude of the wise man[143]: Prov 10 18 10 19 10 20 10 21
10 31–32 14 1.3 14 7 11 13 12 6 12 13–14 12 18–19 12 22 12 23 13 3 15 2 15 4 15 28
19 28 17 20 18 2 21 23 25 11 25 28 29 11 29 20 29 22 Qoh 5 2 10 12 Job 13 5 Ps
37 30 Sir 20 5[144], etc. This theme was also very popular in Egypt[145] (cf. e.g.
The Instructions of Amenemope XXII: 13–14)[146] and in Mesopotamia (cf.
e.g. The Babylonian Counsels of Wisdom 11 21–25)[147]. This ethos of
being reticent must not be understood negatively. It is a positive concept of
being discreet in wise reflection. Obstinate and uncontrolled speech is
characteristic of the *lēṣ* and the *nābāl* who do not respect the divine order
and are not concerned about the chaos they create.

In view of these aspects one can qualify the ethos of wisdom as the
humble subordination to the divine and created order. Subordination to
the created order means in fact re-established order in human conduct[148].
Accordingly man cannot autonomously design his own ethical imperative,
but the ethical imperative heteronomously originates in God, the creator of
order. Thus, wisdom's morality is not autonomous, but on the contrary, it
is diametrically opposed to Greek and philosophical ethics which ascribe
priority to man's reason. Human conscience cannot be the starting point
for knowledge of good and evil[149].

A final aspect of the ethos of wisdom calls for our attention, namely,
the so-called *optimistic*[150] character of the ethos of wisdom. As such it is

---

[143] Cf. the extensive study of Bühlmann, W. op. cit. especially 172ff. and 214ff. and Gese,
H. op. cit. 16.

[144] Cf. Haspecker, J. op. cit. 337ff.

[145] Cf. Brunner, H., Altägyptische Erziehung, 1957, 4ff. 120–122; von Rad, G. op.cit.
118; Fohrer, G., Theologische Grundstrukturen des Alten Testaments, 1972, 122f.;
Hermisson, H.-J. op. cit. 72–73 and Kayatz, C. op. cit. 56.

[146] ANET 424.

[147] Lambert, G., BWL, 99.

[148] K. Barth already implemented the concept of subordination (not exactly in the same
manner as described here) in his special ethics: cf. McKelway, A. J., Scot. Journ. of
Theology 32 (1979), 345–357. Barth seriously tries to define the created and divine order
in view of which he can illuminate the man-woman relationship.

[149] Cf. Vriezen, Th. C. op. cit. 316ff. and our discussion in Chapter 5.

[150] Cf. Hempel, J. op. cit. 187ff.; Fohrer, G. op. cit. 87; Rylaarsdam, J. C., Revelation in the
Jewish Wisdom Literature, 1963, 63; Skladny, U. op. cit. 82 and Ringgren, H., Sprüche,
1962, 45.

undeniable that the wisdom (especially the older wisdom) reflects an optimistic attitude, because it spells out what is good and what is bad; it also indicates which human acts result in good or bad consequences and it lays special emphasis on the outcome of wise and righteous conduct as opposed to foolish and wicked conduct[151]. This optimism of the wisdom interpreted in terms of a strict dogma of act-consequence, would also be irreconcilable with the Jahwistic belief: »Weisheit ist nicht etwa erst vom Jahweglauben zur Lebensfreude befreit, sondern in sich optimistisch, da sie Glück für erreichbar und das jeweils Bessere für erkennbar und vollziehbar hält, welches wiederum dann positives Ergehen aus sich heraussetzt.«[152] Accordingly this optimism is shattered by the criticism of Job and Qohelet.

It must, however, be emphasised, provided that the optimism in the wisdom is understood correctly, that the wisdom of Qohelet and Job do not imply a total break with the older wisdom[153]. Job and Qohelet bring about a real crisis in wisdom and a break with an absolutised act-consequence dogma. If the optimism is understood as the strict causality of act-consequence, then it is obvious that reaction and an eventual break with it will occur.

Firstly, we must emphasise that the »optimism« of the older wisdom is not that of a strict system which one has at his disposal. The limitations and incapability of man are pointed out (cf. Prov 14 2 21 2 20 9 16 2 17 3 20 27 24 12 16 9 16 1 16 33 and 21 31). We have also illustrated previously that the ethos is not an ethos of absolute human sovereignty, but that of subordination to the order of Jahweh (Prov 16 1–3). An absolute system of causality fails in view of the absolute majesty and sovereignty of God. In a rigid system of causality, God himself is bound by the inevitable. Job protested therefore against the dogma of his friends and tries to show them that his suffering and his belief is irreconcilable with such a dogma and a God who must abide by it.

Although the insufficiency and potential danger of the »optimism« of the older wisdom are emphasized by Job and Qohelet, they definitely do not strip so-called »optimism« of all truth.

An »optimism« based on an absolute causality of act-consequence is overcome in Israel by Jahwism[154]. Otherwise one could logically maintain

---

[151] To quote a few: Prov 1 15–16 3 3–4 4 10 10 5 10 11 10 16 10 30 11 5 11 19 12 12 13 22 14 8 14 19 15 7 15 25 15 27 17 5 18 7 21 7 21 13 22 10, etc.

[152] Preuss, H. D. op. cit. 1970, 398.

[153] Cf. Gese, H., Les Sagesses du Proche-Orient Ancien, 1962, 139–151, and Crenshaw, J. L., Studies in Ancient Israel, 1976, 295 ff. Cf. also von Rad's (Weisheit in Israel 148) objections against the optimism-pessimism contrast as a methodological means to determine the difference between the older educational wisdom and the younger theological wisdom. Compare also O. Kaiser's characterization of Qohelet's thought in NZSThK 14 (1972), 22–27.

[154] Cf. par. 4.4.

an absolute optimism founded on the *lex natura* as premise. If the
»optimism« of the Jahweh-oriented wisdom is not stripped of all truth, we
must state positively the sense in which it continues to hold good.

First of all, we must consider that the presumption that obedience to
the wisdom or to the *tôrâ* creates the relation towards Jahweh, is foreign to
the Old Testament. The wisdom's ethos and the *tôrâ*-stipulations lend
substance to and guide towards the materialization of the already existing
relation towards Jahweh. The ethos of the *tôrâ* and that of the wisdom in
mutual relation prescribe the realization of the obedience towards Jahweh.
In the ethos of wisdom nothing is proclaimed but the practical explication
of obedience in the sense that the recognised and comprehensive created
order of God is *the* order for any kind of existence. Real existence is
possible when the knowledge of the created order entails at once the
discipline of obeying that order.

Secondly, we must critically question the common understanding of
the »optimism« in terms of the act-consequence sequence. Is it correct to
believe that the effect of an act brings about the realization of the good or
the bad quality of the act? Good and bad (evil), in other words, correlate
with the realization of the consequences of the act itself[155]. Such an
interpretation occasions real optimism.

An evolutionary conception of time is engrained in the above interpretation. The act-consequence relation must be understood without reference
to temporal development. The act itself is its evil (wickedness) or goodness.
The act itself is expression of the manner (good or evil) in which it is
performed[156]. The act itself is the act against the created order or in
harmony with that order. In the act itself the order is constituted or
violated. When the act in harmony with the order is considered good, this is
not to give vent to over-optimism, but to express that the truth is realized.
The moment in which the human act re-establishes order in harmony with
the created order, the truth of human conduct is realized, but in the
moment of the wicked act the order is violated and chaos is created. The
goodness or evil is not directly connected with the outcome or effect of the
act. The effect or consequence of an act might be misleading, but the judgement of the act itself in as far as it re-establishes or violates the order is
either positive or negative. When this view is turned into an optimistic
dogma (and we cannot reject the fact that in some wisdom circles that did
happen) the quality of the consequence of the act becomes the logical
evaluation of the act itself. Against such a dogma Job and Qohelet protested.

---

[155] Cf. Bauer-Kayatz, Einführung in die alttestamentliche Weisheit, 1969, 29.
[156] Koch, K. op. cit. 1—42 already emphasized the inner connection between the act and its
consequences in his criticism of the dogma of retribution.

Positively we would rather prefer to define the dogma of the wisdom as a positive *realism* rather than as »optimism«. This realism is supported by the knowledge that the created order is not fully at man's disposal and that real obedience is only possible in the humble subordination to the order of God.

To conclude: An absolute system of morality is not provided by the wisdom literature. The theological context of the wisdom is an absolute condition which must be considered when the ethos of the wisdom is defined.

We have tried to make clear that the knowledge expressed in the wisdom is oriented to the created order: Wisdom is the knowledge of the created order and of God himself. This knowledge is not opposed to revelation, but within the sphere of the *yir'at Jahweh* harmonizes with it fully. We are inclined to view the theological context of the wisdom as part and parcel of a theology of creation. In the wisdom it becomes clear that the revelation in the creation (»Schöpfungsoffenbarung«) does not contrast with the revelation of the will of God, otherwise it would have been impossible to identify the wisdom and the *tôrâ*.

Knowledge and ethos do not mutually exclude each other, but presuppose one another. The ethos of wisdom demands an orderly existence in harmony with the created order. Thus, the ethos can be qualified as an ethos of subordination to the divine order. Subordination as an ethical existential re-establishes order. In the act of humble subordination the sovereignty of Jahweh is recognized and substance is given to the state of *šālôm*.

The act-consequence sequence is present in the ethos of the wisdom, but it must not be viewed as an absolute »optimism«, but rather as the realism of wisdom in which the act itself is viewed as re-established order or the violation of order.

Chapter 5: The Ethos as Recognition of the Evil

The reality of evil is prominent in documents of Christianity, but almost always illuminated under the aspect of deliverance from evil. Thus, the evil is discussed as an aspect of soteriology. From various texts in the wisdom literature we will try to clarify certain aspects of the nature of evil and try to define the coherence of evil with the ethical imperative.

The classical psychological definition of evil has been worked out by C. G. Jung[1]. Evil is, according to Jung, a reality which nestles in the psyche. Evil is psychic evil which collaborates in every decision-making process of man. Jung is reluctant to describe the ethical demand as a triumph over evil, although he admits that the self-realization of man includes a victory over evil[2], but then as a psychic achievement. The origin of evil is the libido (psychic dynamic[3]) of man and from here it determines the (negative) emotional reaction. God is accordingly the archetype of the psyche. God is the good and the evil: In other words, good and evil originate in God.

Even in Greek thought it is found that the origin of good and evil is located in the reality of the gods[4], (then understood quite differently than in the psychological approach). Already in Zeus the evil is present. The good and evil are located within the realm of the gods, and it is their prerogative to decide whether the conduct of man is good or evil. Being almost delivered to the judgement of the gods in respect of man's conduct, is described by Theognis as man's fate:

»Weiß doch keiner der Menschen, ob ihm das Ziel seines Handelns
seiner Absicht gemäß gut oder böse gedeiht.
Keinem der Menschen wird, was er sich wünscht, auch zuteil;
denn er verfolget ein Ziel, schwierig und gänzlich unmöglich.
Da wir nichts wissen, treiben Eiteles zwar wir Menschen;
doch die Götter vollenden alles nach ihrem Rat.«[5]

The ethical demand in Greek thought is, however, not postulated in direct opposition to evil as an ontological reality. The ethical code, accor-

---

[1] Cf. the extensive and critical evaluation of Jung's assumption of evil by Beck, I., Das Problem des Bösen und seine Bewältigung, 1976.

[2] Ibid. 46.

[3] Contra Freud's pure sexuality.

[4] Cf. Ricoeur, P. op.cit. (German translation) 247.

[5] Translation of Kaiser, O., Neue Zeitschrift für Systematische Theologie und Religionsphilosophie 14 (1972), 6.

ding to Plato, consists of the realization of the ideas »viewed« by man in his pre-physical existence: Righteous living is the image of the idea of righteousness. By remembrance the realization of the image of the idea is still possible. The ethical reality reflected in the realm of ideas, would soon become changed into an ethical philosophy which finds in the subject (the individual) the origin of all values. This ethical movement connected to the freedom of the individual occurs during the 5—4 century B.C. and, according to Wundt, consists of the following:

»Sie bedeutet eine Erlösung aus dem Zwange der objektiven Welt, an die sich der Mensch bis dahin gekettet sah und unter deren Widersprüchen und Unwerten er zu leiden hatte. Mit seinem Herzblut hatte er sich von ihr losgerungen und in sich selbst den festen Punkt erobert, von dem aus er in Freiheit nach eigenen Normen sein Leben sich gestalten konnte.«[6]

According to Aristotle[7] it is then possible for the subject to realise the highest (ethical) form of happiness in an existence following reason. The smallest aspect of reason realised in ethical conduct is a stage of development towards supreme morality. The highest form of ethical existence is to be found with the philosopher, because in the philosopher the highest function of man, reason, is unfolded. The ethical goodness as an integral part of man is possible.

From the period of Epikur a sceptical movement is introduced. Transcendental and objective norms are rejected and what remains is the value-judgement of the individual and his impressions of the experienced world. For the empirical existence the dominant principle is pleasure (Lust): All values intentionally strived after by man, are reducable to one or another sentiment of pleasure and happiness. Affection and emotion were morally deficient for Plato and Aristotle, but they became the highest principles for Epikur: »das Denken ist selbst gewissermaßen nur noch eine Stimmung, die dauerndste und sicherste, doch wertvoll nur wegen dieses ihres Gefühlscharakters«[8].

According to the Stoic philosophers the ethical demand implies a withdrawal from the empirical world, which is characterized by suffering and emotion. The highest form of morality is realized in the wise man who has achieved total inner freedom through reason.

Reason is the highest form of joy and fortune. Through reason the real nature (morality) of man can be materialized[9]. The basic assumption that the morality of man and his inner nature are congruent and ought to be identical, is evident. It is also clear that the ethical imperative originates in

---

[6] Wundt, Max, Geschichte der Griechischen Ethik, II 1911, 62.

[7] For the Ethics of Aristotle cf. Wundt, M. op.cit. 110ff., and Weischedel, W., Skeptische Ethik, 1975, 17—19.

[8] Wundt, M. op.cit. 188.

[9] Ibid. 228f.

man himself — through reason he knows what is good and bad behaviour. The autonomous imperative moral accordingly figures in the field of epistemology. Even in catholic ethics (the thomistic kind) the ability to distinguish between good and evil is an inherent cognitive ability of man. However, catholic thought normally tries to gloss over the contradiction between an autonomous moral imperative and so-called theonomy[10].

The philosophy of the Stoa (eg. Kleanthes) eventually developed into a kind of pantheistic metaphysics through which reason became almost identical with the cosmos[11].

In Greek thought the ethos appears as a human reality and it demands self-realization — normally by reason. The ethos is not formulated in opposition to a concept of evil. Even according to Augustine the ethos is not absolutely determined by the relation towards God, but also by the inner aspect of goodness in man[12].

In the account of the creation in Gen 1 evil can be identified with the reality of chaos. The creative activity is seen as new order over against chaos[13].

In the story of Adam (Gen 3) the concept of evil is more complex. The problem is: Is the reality of evil presupposed in Gen 3 or is Gen 3 the premise of Israel's experience of evil and guilt? According to M. Buber the story of Gen 3 should not occasion an interpretation of the ethical consciousness of good and bad, but rather »Erkenntnis der Gegensätze: zureichendes Bewußtsein der Gegensätzlichkeit alles innerweltlichen Seins, und das heißt vom biblischen Schöpfungsglauben aus: zureichendes Bewußtsein der in der Schöpfung latenten Gegensätzlichkeit«[14]. Becoming conscious of the »Gegensätzlichkeit«, the latent reality of creation, as a real reality of one's own existence is the result of man's trespass in the garden of Eden. Knowing the »Gegensätze« brings about the factual reality of man's involvement in good and evil (19). The story of Adam, according to Paul Ricoeur[15], presupposes the reality of evil, because evil is simply present in Eden. He considers the story of Adam as the »Mythos der Abweichung«

---

[10] Cf. eg. Korff, W., Theologische Ethik, 1975, 19ff., and his Norm und Sittlichkeit, 1973, 62ff.

[11] Ibid. 252.

[12] Weischedel, W. op. cit. 20 and Rankin, O. S. op. cit. 30. Cf. Geesink, W., Gereformeerde Ethiek, 1931, 157ff., for a cursory and brief look into the history of theological ethics. For Augustine God can in no way be the author of evil.

[13] An assumption quite common in the creation stories of the Ancient Near East. Cf. e.g. The Repulsion of the Dragon from Creation (Egypt), Enuma Eliš (Mesopotamia) and the Baal-Yam conflict in the Ugaritic Literature (Text 68). Cf. also Job 26 10ff. Ps 74 12–17 89 10 f. 104 26 and Is 27 1.

[14] Buber, M., Bilder von Gut und Böse, 1964, 16.

[15] Ricoeur, P. op. cit. 270f. and 294. Rankin, O. S. op. cit. 16ff. even maintains that according to Jahwistic belief, God is the creator of good and evil.

rather than the »Mythos des Falls«[16]. It is, however, remarkable that the Jahwistic writer intends to explain evil by means of a certain event and a certain person[17], without a real discussion of the ontological nature of the evil. One may assume that evil is to be accepted as a latent reality, but it is not explained as a reality which originates in God[18]. In the story of Adam and from the stories of creation it becomes clear that evil is the reality which destroys and violates the order of God[19]. Evil is the reality which subverts a Jahweh-directed existence and tries to exclude man from the grace of God's presence[20].

The Wisdom literature, according to R. Pfeiffer, pictures God as the enemy of evil and the patron of good, because He himself is the absolute good. God's will in this world is directed towards the realization of ethical goodness in every respect. Ethical human conduct must then result in the realization of God's will, which means the realization of ethical goodness. God who is the supreme norm of good is then also the only norm of any form of ethics[21]. One can appreciate Pfeiffer's premise that a non-religious ethics is foreign to the wisdom literature. He however fails to demonstrate in which manner knowledge of the ethical good is mediated to man and in which way the ethical good can be realized in human conduct. The realization of God's will must be made more specific with regard to the ethos of the wisdom.

The preceding was nothing but a fragmentary introduction to the problem of the conception of evil and its impact on any attempt to define an ethos. In the preceding chapter we have tried to define the ethos of wisdom, but now it remains to answer the question as to the starting point of the realization of this ethos. To do so, we have to look at the characterization of evil in the wisdom literature (mainly Proverbs).

An illustrative description of wicked men is to be found in Is 59 7ff. Prov 1 20–33 4 14–17 and Job 27 13–23. The wicked men are directed towards evil in thought and conduct. They violate the rights of innocent people and wherever they go there is havoc, ruin and bloodshed. They are restless in their attempt to create chaos (Prov 4 14ff. and 28 1). They are in direct conflict with the šālôm (Jes 59 8) — they violate the created order. These passages give us a clear picture of the very being of the evil-doers: They represent a reality opposed to that of order and life (cf. Prov 10 21 and 18 7). They work destruction in any form of meaningful existence.

In Prov 30 21–23 four things are listed which disturb the cosmic order and one of these is the foolish man — who lacks wisdom. The wicked men

---

[16] Ibid. 266.
[17] St. Paul (I Cor 15 21ff. and Rom 5 12–21) interpreted the facts accordingly.
[18] In contrast with Greek thought.
[19] Cf. the description of Satan by von Rad, ThWNT II, 74.
[20] Cf. Arenhoevel, D., Ur-Geschichte: Gen 1–11, 1973, 62.
[21] Cf. Pfeiffer, R. op. cit. 43 ff.

operate against the will of God (Prov 28 4) because their hearts are always scheming evil (Prov 4 16 and Prov 2 14f.).

The foolish man belongs to the category of the wicked: both figure in opposition to the ṣaddîq. The fool represents chaos through his stupidity, reluctance and negligence towards orderly existence. He is one easily impressed and caught by evil and wicked men, because he is inconstant and self-assured (Prov 15 7 27 22 29 11 12 15 14 16 28 26). His foolishness brings about his own destruction (Prov 10 21 and 18 7), because he is in fact against God himself (Prov 19 3).

The reality of evil affects the heart, (Prov 16 2 17 9–10 Jer 3 17), the very centre of one's existence. The subjective consciousness of the fool or wicked man might be positive (wise in his own eyes), but to the wise man it is a sign of his arrogance.

The end of the foolish and wicked men is their own destruction (Prov 26 27 and Prov 28 10) and their destination is the reality of meaningless existence — death (Prov 1 19 2 18–19 5 22–23 5 5 7 26 9 18 and Ps 37 9).

The psychology of evil is best explained in Prov 2 16. 5 and 7 with the predication of the zārâ. We have paid attention to the fact that the predication of the zārâ occurs as a motivation of wisdom's demand to obey its instructions[22]. The zārâ in fact figures in direct opposition to wisdom: The zārâ becomes the diametrical opposite of wisdom. This can only be understood from the fact that the zārâ has become symbolized evil[23] — the zārâ is the evil an sich. In the wisdom the zārâ is the best exemplification of evil and its nature. Real wisdom is therefore the avoidance of the zārâ. The loose-living Israelite woman represents a manifestation of the subtle and seductive method by which evil lures one into its power. She operates in the dark (Prov 7 9) — symbol of chaos, and specializes in her psychological approach (Prov 5 3 7 13f.).

Evil reveals itself in its seductive approach and to be caught by evil means death (Prov 2 18–19 5 5 and 7 27). Once in its power, escape is impossible (Prov 7 22–23 and Is 13 23).

Thus, the wisdom literature represents evil as the reality opposed to wisdom: It is the reality which subverts and violates the order of Jahweh and in the end destroys meaningful existence. The evil affects the real existence of people and those caught up by it, become devoted citizens of the state of chaos and evil.

---

[22] Cf. our discussion of the predication as motivation in par. 3.1.5.

[23] Cf. the various explanations and interpretations of the zārâ: Boström, G., Proverbien-studien: Die Weisheit und das fremde Weib in Sprüche 1–9, 1935; Snijders, L. A., The meaning of zr in the Old Testament, OTS 10, 1954, 1–154; Lang, B., Die weisheitliche Lehrrede, 1972, 88–96; Toy, C. H. op. cit. 103ff.; McKane, W. op. cit. 285; Gemser, B. op.cit. 5ff.; Perdue, L. G., Wisdom and Cult, 1977, 146–153; Rankin, O. S. op.cit. 259ff., and Humbert, P., Opuscules d'un Hébraïsant, 1958, 111–118.

Wisdom is the reality opposed to evil reality and therefore wisdom is achieved in avoidance of the evil. The wise man not only understands his »way« (Prov 14 8), but he also has knowledge of the manifestations of evil (Prov 21 12 and 23 3). To obey wise instruction is to avoid evil (cf. Prov 20 26 24 20ff. 23 3 26 24–26 27 12 24 1–2 24 19–20 21 12). In other biblical literature the same idea that to turn away from evil is to step towards life (Ez 33 14–15 and Ps 34 13–15), occurs. That clearly presupposes that man knows what evil is. It was a general assumption that the wise knows the »ways« of evil and not-knowing is even worse than the evil deed itself (cf. Am 3 10 and Is 1 13). Evil must be hated and avoided (Am 5 15 Deut 13 6 17 7 21 21 24 7, etc.) and it is made clear in the Psalms (cf. Ps 15 2f. and 24 4f.) that only those who refrain from doing evil will participate in the liturgy of God.

From the various texts mentioned above, we get the impression that the wisdom evaluates existence ontologically in a positive and negative sense: Positive existence is to live in obedience to wise instruction and therefore in harmony with the created order; Negative existence is accomplished within the reality of evil[24], which is in direct opposition to the order of God.

Evil, according to wisdom has it in itself to manifest itself and that these manifestations of evil are recognizable to the wise man. The wise man to whom the created order of God is revealed, is in a position to recognize the evil through its acts of promoting chaos and violating the order of Jahweh.

Accordingly one of the most peculiar characteristics of the wisdom now emerges: The ethical demand (the ethos) of wisdom is represented and formulated in opposition to the recognized anti-pole of wisdom, that is to say, evil. The ethos of wisdom is formulated positively only in coherence with the recognition of its (wisdom's) negation.

This idea already seems present in Prov 14 16: »The wise man fears and avoids evil, the fool is rash and presumptuous«.

The fear of the wise man is co-ordinately juxtaposed with the avoidance of evil. A problem exists however, as to how to interpret the *yārēʾ*: Is it merely to be »afraid« of the evil or does it imply the religious principle as the basic manner of conduct of the wise man? In view of parallel texts (cf. Prov 16 6 3 7 8 13 and Job 28 28) the latter seems preferable, but the two aspects mentioned do not necessarily exclude each other. The attitude of being afraid of evil is obviously a realization of the religious principle of *yārēʾ*[25].

---

[24] It is not only a power of the inner psyche, but rather a reality (according to Gen 1–3) opposed to the created order of God.

[25] Interpreted in coherence with *yirʾat Jahweh*.

There can be no doubt that in Prov 16 6 the religious principle of wisdom is qualified as avoidance of evil:

> »By kindliness and loyalty atonement is made for sin,
> with the fear of Jahweh goes avoidance of evil«.   (JB)

The religious principle (religion) in which real wisdom is founded, is understood as the avoidance of evil. Real belief and wise conduct[26] are realized in opposition to and in avoidance of evil. The religious principle is not brought forward in the realization of the *good* as a given possibility in man, but in opposition to the reality of evil. Therefore, real wisdom, which is only realized in the framework of the *yir'at Jahweh*, is a guardian to keep one from the way of evil (Prov 2 10–15 and Job 28 28)[27]. The ethos of wisdom is understood as the avoidance of evil. The avoidance of evil is the realization of the existence of the wise man.

In Prov 3 7[28] the following explication of the principle of humility is found:

> »Do not think of yourself as wise,
> fear Jahweh and avoid evil,«

Real wisdom is not present in proud self-esteem (the hybris), but in the *yir'at Jahweh* as the religious principle. And again the religious principle is co-ordinately linked with the world and existence in general: The juxtaposition of the religious principle with the *sûr mērā'* follows from the assumption that the ethical realization of the religious principle is an existence in avoidance of evil. The motivation of this proverb (v. 8) makes it clear that the ethical aspect of the religious principle (*yir'at Jahweh*) cannot be excluded. The realization of the *yir'at Jahweh* as the ethical avoidance of evil brings about physical health and real life.

The *yir'at Jahweh*'s ethical bearing receives further explication in Prov 8 13:

> »The fear of Jahweh is hatred of evil:
> I hate pride and haughtiness,
> evil conduct and twisted speech.«[29]

Pride and haughtiness of man before Jahweh is considered to be a manifestation of evil and indicative of a contemptuous attitude towards Jahweh[30]. In Sir 15 8 it is also made evident that those who fear the Lord (15 1) will stand far removed from pride.

---

[26] Belief and ethics are not mutually exclusive.

[27] One of the major characteristics of Job as a wise man is his avoidance of evil (Job 1 1).

[28] Pfeiffer, R. op. cit. 44 maintains that this proverb supports the presumption that God himself is the enemy of evil!

[29] McKane, W. op. cit. 222.

[30] Cf. Jes 2 11.

Thus, the *yir'at Jahweh* in its ethical implication is realized in opposition to and in the recognition of evil. The ethos of wisdom starts with the recognition of the evil. Von Rad[31] shares this assumption, but maintains that the nature of evil is not clarified. He therefore emphasizes the good, rather then the evil as the foundation of wisdom's ethos: »Das Gute wurde von ihm (Israel) einfach als eine Macht erfahren, als etwas schlechthin Lebensbestimmenden, etwas täglich Erfahrenes und auch Wirksames, also als etwas Vorhandenes, über das so wenig zu diskutieren war, wie über Licht und Finsternis.«[32] C. Nink tries to define the good with reference to the *imago Dei*: »Gutsein im ursprünglichen Sinn heißt seinem Subjekt, dessen Wesen, Sinn und innere urbildlicher Norm dessen Ziel, Ordnung, sinnvoller Naturtendenz und finaler Norm entsprechen.«[33] In reference to the *imago Dei* as principle it means: »Der Mensch soll seiner gottebenbildlichen Natur, Einstellung, Haltung und Tendenz sowie ihrer naturgegebenen richtig, gut und zielklar erfolgenden persönlich – autoritativen Steuerung entsprechend handeln.«[34] The ethically *good* act is then possible when it is accomplished in voluntary obedience to the created order of Jahweh and therefore according to the God-given nature of man[35]. It is a typically Augustinian approach to explain the ethically good act on the assumption that man is basically created good. The act in accordance with the created goodness of man is the ethically good act. This conception is not present in the wisdom literature. Wise and ethical conduct, according to the wisdom literature, is not the realization of man's inherent goodness, but it is the avoidance of evil. Against Von Rad it must be maintained that we do find a charaterization of evil in the wisdom literature. Evil is not merely morally bad conduct, but evil is reality in violation of the created order of God. Knowledge of evil is reveales to the wise man within the sphere of the *yir'at Jahweh*. Evil is therefore not the »evil« outcome of the human act or behaviour and it is not merely related to the attitude in which the act is committed, but the act itself[36] is evil in as far as it violates the created order of God. It is recognition of evil which evokes »good« and ethically responsible conduct. The accomplishment of the ethical demand is the realization of one's god-given existence, not in

---

[31] Von Rad, G. op. cit. 106.

[32] Ibid. 106.

[33] Nink, C., Metaphysik des sittlich Guten, 1955, 2.

[34] Ibid. 36–37.

[35] Ibid. 17. The *imago Dei*, according to M. Buber op. cit. 16–17 reflects the »Gegensätzlichkeit« of human existence: Good and bad as the opposite realities of human existence, although irreconcilable in man, are the image of God in which the »Gegensätzlichkeit« is a positive reality.

[36] Van Oyen, H. op. cit. 67 correctly acknowledges the importance of the act itself, but creates an artificial differentiation between the act and the good or bad background of the act.

accordance with the created nature of man or in accordance with the reason[37] of man, but in accordance with the consciousness of man's own evil and in opposition to this evil.[38] It is only possible through an existence in wisdom —not as a merely cognitive human ability, but as a gift of Jahweh within the religious principle of the *yir'at Jahweh*. Thus, the recognition of evil is the starting point for the ethos of wisdom. Over against evil the ethos of wisdom means the recreation and re-affirmation of created order. In as far as ethical conduct means re-affirmed order, which holds forth the promise of life[39], it gives substance to the *šālôm*.

Salvation and the state of »orderly« existence is positively defined only in as far as it is the anti-thesis of evil. It almost seems as if the truth and reality of salvation is too great for man's reason and too overwhelming than that it could be explained positively. Therefore, the ethical realization of salvation (in accordance with the created order), is the avoidance of evil. Salvation is the state contrasting with the state of evil. A very similar idea is encountered in Jeremiah when he proclaims salvation as a »turning away from« (*šûb*). Jeremiah too sees salvation as the contrary of the state of wrong-doing and evil.

It is likely that the symmetry of thoughts so prominent in the wisdom literature, as also comparison, functions also in wisdom's concept of truth (salvation). Truth is constituted in the symmetry of its negative and positive poles. In other words the truth of salvation is not positively formulated as such. Its meaning is only understood in recognition of its opposite, of evil as evil.

The truth of man's existence is determined by this coherence of contrasts, viz. of evil and salvation. The truth of wisdom's ethos cannot be materialized without awareness of its negation as represented in evil. That is why wisdom's ethos starts with the recognition of evil. The truth is supported by the symmetry of the negative and the positive reality of existence.

If this idea holds true, it entails that truth is not at man's disposal, but instead becomes intelligible and becomes real in one's existence the moment its negation (that is, evil) is disclosed (revealed) unto man. Without God's revelation there can be no real ethos, because revelation is the revelation of man's ethos in service of the purpose of creation. Truth of existence (real life) is realized in opposition to evil, which is reality in violation of God's created order and in opposition to the truth of God's reality and to God himself.

---

[37] Against the ethos of the Greek philosophy.

[38] According to Buber, M. op. cit. 34–36 and 56ff., the evil and the good are the two existential possibilities of man. Both aspects must be realized in true existence, but the good nor necessarily in contrast to the evil.

[39] Cf. the Extensive study of Schmitt, E., Leben in den Weisheitsbüchern Job, Sprüche und Jesus Sirach, 1954, especially 122ff.

The ideas advanced here have been presented in only a preliminary and fragmentary manner. Extensive research is required to arrive at a complete understanding as to why salvation is described in opposition to evil. A penetrating study comparing the various concepts and traditions of salvation of the Old Testament is urgently needed. If it is found that salvation is always spoken of in the context of its negation, then the consequences thereof for the concept of salvation will require attention. That would imply renewed examination of the concepts of sin, salvation and truth.

Concluding Statements

Since a brief summary was given at the end of each Chapter and subdivision, we can restrict ourselves to a few concluding statements of the results of our enquiry.

Structural and Form-Critical Features

1. The admonition in Proverbs occurs in coherence with a motivation. This coherence must be determined from grammatical and semantic features.

2. Proof for the view that the motivation is the result of the educational functioning of the admonition has been found to be insufficient. The coherence admonition-motivation demonstrates the unity of form and content and gives realization to an inner logic which is as original as the admonition itself.

3. The admonition may be formulated positively by means of an Imperative or Jussive and negatively by means of a Vetitive or Prohibitive. The Prohibitive in Proverbs does not constitute a genre different from the genre of the Vetitive.

4. The frequency of admonitions is the highest in those collections with an explicit instructional character such as Coll. C. and A. This is not proof of a gradual and evolutionary development from the wisdom saying towards the admonition.

5. Linguistically we can describe the admonition as follows: the admonition consists of an admonitory element, in the grammatical form of an Imperative, Jussive, Vetitive or Prohibitive and a motivative element, which might vary in grammatical form, length and explication. The introductory particles of the motivative clauses vary and are not necessarily connected with the positive or negative character of the admonitory element.

The Ethos of the (Wisdom) Admonition

1. The ethos of the wisdom can be described successfully, provided that the function and role of the motivation is duly considered and that the inner logic of the coherence admonition-motivation is grasped. This inner logic reveals to us the intention of the admonition and as such constitutes the authority of the admonition. The authority of the admonition does not centre in the various institutions by which wisdom (admonitions) are proclaimed nor in the authoritative officials who represent the various institutions.

2. The motivation of the admonition is not just a didactic device or the result of the application of logical principles to the admonition, but it is a fixed structural feature which illuminates the validity and truth of the ethos of the admonition. This ethos is clarified by the reasonable, explanatory, dissuasive and promissory character of the motivation. Thus, the intention of the motivation is indeed educative, but it does not necessarily originate in an educational institution.

3. A distinction between the law and the codification of the law must be maintained in order to determine the relationship between the *tôrâ* and the wisdom.

4. The identification of law and wisdom in the later wisdom literature can be explained from the inherent identity in ethos and content of both.

5. The identification of law and wisdom in the tradition makes clear that the revelation of God's will (in the *tôrâ*) and knowledge of the created order are complementary and not diametrically opposed.

6. Although the concept of the *yir'at Jahweh* might be the result of the theological re-interpretation of wisdom, it nevertheless represents the central religious principle in the wisdom literature. The *yir'at Jahweh* is the religious existential of ethical conduct.

7. The presence of the conception of the *yir'at Jahweh* does not allow us to interpret wisdom as natural theology.

8. The theological context of wisdom and wisdom's ethos are inseparable.

9. Wisdom's limits and goal is to be found in the *yir'at Jahweh*.

10. The created order appears to be the central theme. Knowledge of this order embodies an immanent ethos of subordination to this order. Subordination to the created order means the re-affirmation of order in human conduct.

11. The so-called »optimism« of the wisdom, interpreted as an absolute causality of the act-consequence sequence, is based on an unjustifiable linear time conception.

12. The motivation and starting point of wisdom's ethos is the recognition of evil. It is an ethos diametrically opposed to evil and does not result from the goodness of man or the superior functions of human reason.

In this enquiry we have tried to determine the importance of the motivation of the admonition and its contribution to an understanding of the ethos of wisdom.

We sincerely hope that the study will occasion further enquiry about both wisdom's ethos and its motivation and about the ethos of the other Old Testament traditions. Thorough investigation is required for a satisfactory elucidation of the symmetry of thought found in wisdom and its bearing on wisdom's conception of truth. Provision of a justified view of the conception of truth will shed more light on the ethos of wisdom as well as on the tradition in its entirety.

Further study is required to demonstrate the implementation of the principles of the ethos of wisdom in the particular ethics of family, marriage, education, religion, state-affairs, personal possession, social behaviour, etc. Recognition of the principles basic to wisdom's ethos will keep us from treating the various topics of wisdom's ethics as if it were a strict system of morality.

Bibliography

Albright, W. F., Some Canaanite-Phoenician Sources of Hebrew Wisdom, VTS 3, 1955, 1–15.

Alonso-Schökel, L., Motivos sapienciales y de alianza en Gen 2–3, Bibl 43 (1962), 295–315.

Alt, A., Die Ursprünge des israelitischen Rechts, KS zur Geschichte des Volkes Israel, I 1952, 278–332.

Andrae, T., Rätsel, RGG² IV, 1685.

Andersen, F. I., Israelite Kinship Terminology and Social Structure, Bible Transl. 20 (1969), 29–39.

Anthes, R., Lebensregeln und Lebensweisheit der Alten Ägypter, 1933.

Arenhoevel, D., Ur-Geschichte: Gen 1–11, 1973².

Audet, J-P., Origines comparées de la double tradition de la loi et de la sagesse dans le proche-orient ancien, 25th International Congress of Orientalists, 1960, Moscow, 352–357.

Bauckmann, E. G., Die Proverbien und die Sprüche des Jesus Sirach: Eine Untersuchung zum Strukturwandel der israelitischen Weisheitslehre, ZAW 72 (1960) 33–63.

Bauer, J. B., Encore une fois Proverbes VIII 22, VT 8 (1958) 91–92.

Baumgärtel, D. F., Eigenart der alttestamentlichen Frömmigkeit, 1931.

Baumgartner, W., The Wisdom Literature, in: The Old Testament and Modern Study (ed. H. H. Rowley), 1952, 210–237.

Baumgartner, W., Die literarischen Gattungen in der Weisheit des Jesus Sirach, ZAW 34 (1914), 161–198.

Baumgartner, W., Israelitische und altorientalische Weisheit, 1933.

Bea, A., Der Zahlenspruch im Hebräischen und Ugaritischen, Bibl 21 (1940), 196–198.

Beaucamp, E., Man's Destiny in the Book of Wisdom, 1970.

Beck, I., Das Problem des Bösen und seine Bewältigung. 1976.

Becker, J., Gottesfurcht im Alten Testament, 1965.

Bernhardt, K. H., Die gattungsgeschichtliche Forschung am AT als exegetische Methode, Ergebnisse und Grenzen, 1956.

Das Problem der altorientalischen Königsideologie im Alten Testament, VTS 8, 1961.

Bjørndalen, A. J., Form und Inhalt des motivierenden Mahnspruches, ZAW 82 (1970), 347–361.

Boecker, H. J., Redeformen des Rechtslebens im Alten Testament, 1964.

Boston, J., The Wisdom Influence upon the Song of Moses, JBL 87 (1968) 198–202.

Boström, G., Proverbienstudien: Die Weisheit und das fremde Weib in Sprüche 1–9, 1935.

Brunner, H., Die Weisheitsliteratur, Ägyptologie, Handbuch der Orientalistik, 1/2 1952.
Gerechtigkeit als Fundament des Thrones, VT 8 (1958), 426–428.
Altägyptische Erziehung, 1957.

Buber, M., Bilder von Gut und Böse, 1964³.

Bühlmann, W., Vom rechten Reden und Schweigen, Studien zu Prov 10–31, 1976.

Bultmann, R., Die Geschichte der synoptischen Tradition, 1964⁶.

Burrows, M., Old Testament Ethics and the Ethics of Jesus, in: Essays in Old Testament Ethics (ed. J. L. Crenshaw), 1974, 288 ff.

Buss, M. J., The Idea of Sitz im Leben – History and Critique, ZAW 90 (1978), 157–171.

Cazelles, H., A propos d'une phrase de H. H. Rowley, VTS 3, 1955, 26–32.

Childs, B. S., Isaiah and the Assyrian Crisis, SBT 2/3, 1967, 129–136.

Crenshaw, J. L., Studies in Ancient Israelite Wisdom, 1976.

    Wisdom, in: Old Testament Form Criticism, (ed. J. H. Hayes), 1977², 225–264.

    Method in Determining Wisdom Influence upon Historical Literature, JBL 88 (1969), 129–142.

    Popular Questioning of the Justice of God in Ancient Israel, in: Studies in Ancient Israelite Wisdom (ed. J. L. Crenshaw), 1976, 289–304.

Dahood, M., Canaanite-Phoenician Influence in Qoheleth, Biblica 33 (1952), 30–52.

    Northwest Semitic Philology and Job, in: The Bible in Current Catholic Thought, 1962, 55–74.

    Proverbs and Northwest Semitic Philology, 1963.

David, Y., Simsons Rätsel nach der Auffassung des Moses Hayyim Luzzatto, Semitics 5 (1977), 32–35.

De Boer, P. A. H., »The Counsellor«, VTS 3, 1955, 42–56.

De Buck, A., Het Religieus karakter der Oudste Egyptische Wijsheid, NThT 21 (1932) 322–349.

Deist, F., Die Betekenissfeer van die leksikale morfeem /-y-r-'-/ in die Profetiese Boeke van die Ou Testament. Unpublished Dissertation, Stellenbosch, 1971.

Delitzsch, F., Biblical Commentary on the Proverbs of Solomon, 1872.

De Vaux, R., Ancient Israel; its life and institutions, 1961.

Drubbel, A., Wijsheid, uit de grondtekst vertaald en uitgelegd, 1957.

Dürr, L., Das Erziehungswesen im Alten Testament und im Antiken Orient, in: Mitteilungen der Vorderasiatisch-Aegyptischen Gesellschaft 36/2, 1932.

Eichhorn, J. G., Einleitung in das Alte Testament, 1824⁴.

Eichrodt, W., Theologie des Alten Testaments, I 1957⁵.

Eissfeldt, O., The Old Testament: an Introduction, 1966².

    Der Maschal im Alten Testament, 1913.

Emerton, J. A., Wisdom, in: Tradition and Interpretation (ed. G. W. Anderson), 1979, 214–237.

Erman, A., Die Literatur der alten Ägypter, 1923 (= The Literature of the Ancient Egyptians, 1927).

Falkenstein, A., Der Sohn des Tafelhauses, WO I (1948), 172–186.

Feinberg, Ch. L., Ugaritic Literature and the Book of Job, Diss. Baltimore, 1945.

Fensham, F. C., Exodus, 1970.

    Widow, Orphan and the Poor in Ancient Near Eastern Legal and Wisdom Literature, JNES 21 (1962), 129–139.

    The Change of the Situation of a Person in Ancient Near Eastern and Biblical Wisdom Literature, AION 31 (1971), 156–164.

Fichtner, J., Die altorientalische Weisheit ih ihrer israelitisch-jüdischen Ausprägung, 1933.

Fohrer, G., Theologische Grundstrukturen des Alten Testaments, 1972.

    (E. Sellin) Einleitung in das Alte Testament, 1965¹⁰.

Forman, C., The Context of Biblical Wisdom, Hibbert Journal 60 (1962), 125–132.

Frye, J. B., The use of māšāl in the Book of Job, Semitics 5 (1977), 59–66.

Fuss, W., Tradition und Komposition im Buche Jesus Sirach (Dissertation Tübingen), 1962.

Galling, K., Kohelet-Studien, ZAW 50 (1932), 276–299.

Geesink, W., Gereformeerde Ethiek, 1931.

Gemser, B., Sprüche Salomos, 1963.
   The Importance of the Motive Clause in the Old Testament Law, VTS 1, 1953, 50–66.
Gerleman, G., The Septuagint Proverbs as a Hellenistic document, OTS 8, 1950, 15–27.
Gerstenberger E., Wesen und Herkunft des apodiktischen Rechts, 1965.
Gese, H., Vom Sinai zum Zion, Alttestamentliche Beiträge zur Biblischen Theologie, 1974.
   Zur Biblischen Theologie, 1977.
   Lehre und Wirklichkeit in der alten Weisheit, 1958.
   Weisheit, RGG³ VI, 1574–1577; Weisheitsdichtung, RGG VI, 1577–1582.
   Beobachtungen zum Stil alttestamentlicher Rechtssätze, ThLZ 85 (1960), 147–150.
   Die Krisis der Weisheit bei Koheleth, in: Les Sagesses du Proche-Orient Ancien 1963,
   139–157.
Gispen, W. H., De Spreuke van Salomo, I 1952, II 1954.
Goldingay, J., The »Salvation History« Prspective and the »Wisdom« Perspective within the
   context of Biblical Theology, The Evangelical Quarterly, 51 (1979), 194–207.
Gordis, R., Quatations in Wisdom Literature, JQR 30 (1939), 123–147.
Gordon, E. I., The Sumerian Proverb Collections, JAOS 74 (1954), 82–85.
   Sumerian Animal Proverbs and Fables, Collection Five, JCS 12 (1958), 1–21 and 43–75.
   Sumerian Proverbs, 1959.
Grumach, I., Untersuchungen zur Lebenslehre des Amenemope, 1972.
Harrington, W., The Wisdom of Israel, IrTQ 30 (1963), 311–325.
Hasel, G. F., The Problem of the Centre in the Old Testament Theology, ZAW 86 (1974),
   65–82.
   Old Testament Theology: Basic issues in the current Debate, 1972.
Haspecker, J., Gottesfurcht bei Jesus Sirach, 1967.
Haupt, P., Koheleth oder Weltschmerz in der Bibel, 1905.
Heering, H. J., Is er een eigen christelijke Ethiek? (Ethiek als Waagstuk – in hon. of Dr E. L.
   Smelik), 1969, 39–50.
Hempel, J., Das Ethos des Alten Testaments, 1938.
   Pathos und Humor in der israelitischen Erziehung, in BZAW 77, 1958, 63–81.
Hengel, M., Judentum und Hellenismus, 1973².
Herbert, A. S., The Parable (maschal) in the Old Testament, SJT 7 (1954), 180–196.
Hermisson, H-J., Studien zur israelitischen Spruchweisheit, 1968.
   Weisheit und Geschichte, in: Probleme biblischer Theologie (FS G. von Rad), 1971,
   136–154.
Hoffmann, H. W., Form-Funktion-Intention, ZAW 82 (1970), 341–346.
Hubbard, D. A., The Wisdom Movement and Israel's Covenant Faith, Tyndale Bulletin 17
   (1966), 3–33.
Hudal, Alois, Die religiösen und sittlichen Ideen des Spruchbuches, 1914.
Hulsbosch, A., Sagesse creatrice et educatrice, Augustinianum 1 (1961), 217–235 and 433–451;
   2 (1962), 5–39.
Humbert, P., Les adjectifs zar et nokri et la »femme étrangère« des Proverbes bibliques, in:
   Opuscules d'un Hébraïsant, 1958, 111–118.
   La »femme étrangère« du livre des Proverbes, Revue des Etudes Sémitiques 6 (1937)
   49–64.
Johnson, A. R., מָשָׁל, VTS 3, 1955, 162–169.
Jolles, A., Einfache Formen, 1958².
Kaiser, O., Einleitung in das Alte Testament, 1975³.
   Der Mensch unter dem Schicksal, NZSThR 14 (1972), 1–28.
   Die Begründung der Sittlichkeit im Buche Jesus Sirach, ZThK 55 (1958), 51–63.

Kayatz, C. B., Einführung in die alttestamentliche Weisheit, 1969.
   Studien zu Proverbien 1—9, 1966.
Keller, Carl-A., Zum sogenannten Vergeltungsglauben im Proverbienbuch, in: Beiträge zur alttestamentlichen Theologie (FS W. Zimmerli), 1977, 223—238.
Kessler, W., Die literarische historische und theologische Problematik des Dekalogs, VT 7 (1957), 1—16.
Klostermann, A., Schulwesen im alten Israel (in FS Th. Zahn), 1908, 193—232.
Koch, K., Gibt es ein Vergeltungsdogma im alten Testament, ZThK 52 (1955), 1—42, and in: Um das Prinzip der Vergeltung in Religion und Recht des Alten Testaments (ed. Koch, K.), 1972, 130—180.
   The Growth of the Biblical Tradition, 1969.
Korff, W., Theologische Ethik, 1975.
   Norm und Sittlichkeit. Untersuchungen zur Logik der normativen Vernunft, 1973.
Kovacs, B. W., Is there a Class-Ethic in Proverbs?, in: Essays in Old Testament Ethics (ed. J. L. Crenshaw), 1974, 171—189.
Kramer, S. N., »Schooldays«. A Sumerian Composition Relating to the Education of a Scribe, JAOS 69 (1949), 199—215.
Kraus, F. R., Vom mesopotamischen Menschen der altbabylonischen Zeit und seiner Welt, 1973.
Kraus, H-J., Die Verkündigung der Weisheit, 1951.
Kuhn, G., Beiträge zur Erklärung des Salomonischen Spruchbuches, 1931.
Kutsch, E., Verheißung und Gesetz. Untersuchungen zum sogenannten »Bund« im Alten Testament. 1973.
   Gesetz und Gnade. Probleme des alttestamentlichen Bundesbegriffs, ZAW 79 (1967), 18—35.
Lambert, W. G., Babylonian Wisdom Literature, 1960.
Lampartner, H., Das Buch der Weisheit, 1975³.
Lang, B., Die weisheitliche Lehrrede, 1972.
   Frau Weisheit, Deutung einer biblischen Gestalt, 1975.
   Schule und Unterricht im alten Israel, in: La Sagesse de l'Ancient Testament, 1979, 186—201.
Langacker, R. W., Language and its Structure, 1968.
Lévêque, L., Le contrepoint théologique apporté par la reflexion sapientielle, in: Questions Disputees d'Ancient Testament (ed. Brekelmans, c.), 183—202.
Liedke, G., Gestalt und Bezeichnung alttestamentlicher Rechtssätze, 1971.
Limbeck, M., Die Ordnung des Heils. Untersuchungen zum Gesetzesverständnis des Frühjudentums, 1970.
Lindblom, J., Wisdom in the Old Testament Prophets, VTS 3, 1955, 193—204.
Loader, J. A., Polariteit in die Denke van Qohelet, Diss. Pretoria, 1973.
   Different Reactions of Job and Qoheleth to the Doctrine of Retribution, OTWSA 15—16, 1972—73, 43—48.
Løgstrup, K. E., Die ethische Forderung, 1968.
Loretz, O., Zur Darbietungsform der »Ich-Erzählung« im Buch Qohelet, CBQ 25 (1963), 46—59.
Marböck, J., Weisheit im Wandel. Untersuchungen zur Weisheitstheologie bei Ben Sira. 1971.
   Gesetz und Weisheit. Zum Verständnis des Gesetzes bei Jesus Ben Sira, BZ 20 (1976) 1—21.

Marzal, A., Gleanings from the Wisdom of Mari, 1976.
McCartney, C. E., The Parables of the Old Testament, 1955.
McCarthy, D. J., Treaty and Covenant, 1963.
    Old Testament Covenant: A Survey of Current Opinions. 1972.
McKane, W., Proverbs, 1970.
McKelway, A. J., The Concept of Subordination in Barth's Special Ethics, in Scot. Journ. of
    Theol. 32 (1979), 345−357.
McKenzie, J. L., Reflections on Wisdom, JBL 86 (1967), 1−9.
Mettinger, T. N.D., Solomonic State Officials, 1971.
Meulli, K., Herkunft und Wesen der Fabel, SAV 50 (1954), 65−93.
Meyer, E., Ursprung und Anfänge des Christentums, II 1921.
Morenz, S., Feurige Kohlen auf das Haupt, ThLZ 78 (1953) 187−192.
Mowinckel, S., Psalms and Wisdom, VTS 3, 1955, 205−224.
    Zur Geschichte der Dekaloge, ZAW 55 (1937), 218−235.
Müller, H-P., Der Begriff »Rätsel« im Alten Testament, VT 20 (1970), 465−489.
Munch, P. A., Die jüdischen »Weisheitspsalmen« und ihr Platz im Leben, OA 15 (1936) 112−
    140.
Murphy, R. E., Introduction to the Wisdom Literature of the Old Testament, 1965.
    Assumptions and Problems in Old Testament Wisdom Research, CBQ 29 (1967),
    407−418.
    Form-criticism and Wisdom Literature, CBQ 31 (1969), 475−483.
Nel, P. J., The Concept »Father« in the Wisdom Literature of the Ancient Near East, JNSL 5
    (1977), 53−66.
Nink, C., Metaphysik des sittlich Guten, 1955.
Nissen, A., Gott und der Nächste im antiken Judentum. 1974.
Noth, M., Die Gesetze im Pentateuch. Ihre Voraussetzungen und ihr Sinn. Gesammelte
    Studien zum AT, 1957.
    Die Bewährung von Salomos »göttlicher Weisheit«, VTS 3, 1955, 225−237.
Oesterley, W. O. E., The Book of Proverbs, 1929.
Ogden, G. S., Qoheleth's use of the »Nothing is Better«-form. JBL 98 (1979), 339−350.
Olivier, J. P. J., Schools and Wisdom Literature, JNSL 4 (1975), 49−60.
    The Old Babylonian Mešarum-Edict and the Old Testament, Dissertation Stellenbosch,
    1978.
Oosterhoff, B. J., De Vreze des Heren in het Oude Testament, 1949.
Oppenheim, A. L., Ancient Mesopotamia, 1964.
Overholt, T. W., Commanding the Prophets: Amos and the Problem of Prophetic Authority,
    CBQ 41 (1979), 517−532.
Perdue, L. G., Wisdom and Cult, 1977.
Peters, N., Das Buch Jesus Sirach oder Ecclesiasticus, 1913.
Petuchowski, J., A Note on W. Kessler's »Problematik des Dekalogs«, VT 7 (1957) 397ff.
Pfeiffer, R., Die religiös-sittliche Weltanschauung des Buches der Sprüche, 1897.
    The Fear of God, IEJ 5 (1955), 41−48.
    The Oldest Decalogue, JBL 43 (1924), 294−310.
Postel, J., Form and Function of the Motive Clause in Prov 10−29, Diss. Iowa, 1976.
Preuss, H. D., Jahwes Antwort an Hiob und die sogenannte Hiobliteratur des alten Vorderen
    Orients, in: Beiträge zur alttestamentlichen Theologie (FS W. Zimmerli) 1977, 323−343.
    Erwägungen zum theologischen Ort alttestamentlicher Weisheitsliteratur, EvTh 30
    (1970), 393−417.

Alttestamentliche Weisheit in christlicher Theologie?, in: Questions Disputées d'Ancient Testament (ed. Brekelmans, C.), 1974, 165–181.

Priest, J. F., Where is Wisdom to be Placed? JBR 31 (1963), 275–282.

Pritchard, J. B., Ancient Near Eastern Texts Relating to the Old Testament, 1974³.

Procksch, O., Theologie des Alten Testaments, 1950.

Rankin, O. S., Israel's Wisdom Literature: Its Bearing on Theology and the History of Religion, 1936.

Reichling, A., Das Problem der Bedeutung in der Sprachwissenschaft, 1963, Univ. Innsbruck.

Rendtorff, R., Geschichtliches und weisheitliches Denken im Alten Testament, in: Beiträge zur alttestamentlichen Theologie (FS W. Zimmerli), 1977, 344–353.

Die Gesetze in der Priesterschrift, 1954.

Richter, H., Die Naturweisheit des Alten Testaments im Buche Hiob, ZAW 70 (1958), 1–20.

Richter, W., Recht und Ethos. Versuch einer Ortung des weisheitlichen Mahnspruches, 1966.

Exegese als Literaturwissenschaft. Entwurf einer alttestamentlichen Literaturtheorie und Methodologie, 1971.

Rickenbacker, O., Weisheitsperikopen bei Ben Sira, 1973.

Ricoeur, P., The Symbolism of Evil, 1969.

Ringgren, H., Word and Wisdom, Studies in the Hypostatization of Divine Qualities and Functions in the Ancient Near East. 1947.

Ringgren, H. and Zimmerli, W., Sprüche/Prediger, 1962.

Roth, W. M. W., Numerical Sayings in the Old Testament, 1965, VTS 13.

Rücker, H., Die Begründungen der Weisungen Jahwes im Pentateuch. 1973.

Rylaarsdam, J. C., Revelation in the Jewish Wisdom Literature, 1946.

Sauer, G., Die Sprüche Agurs, 1963.

Scott, R. B. Y., Proverbs. Ecclesiastes, 1965.

Solomon and the Beginnings of Wisdom in Israel, VTS 3, 1955, 262–279.

Schmid, H. H., Wesen und Geschichte der Weisheit, 1966.

Gerechtigkeit als Weltordnung, 1968.

šālôm, »Frieden« im Alten Orient und im Alten Testament, 1971.

Schmidt, J., Studien zur Stilistik der alttestamentlichen Spruchliteratur, 1936.

Schmidt, W. H., Überlieferungsgeschichtliche Erwägungen zur Komposition des Dekalogs, VTS 22, 1972, 201–220.

Die Schöpfungsgeschichte der Priesterschrift, 1967.

Schmitt, E., Leben in den Weisheitsbüchern Hiob, Sprüche und Jesus Sirach. 1954.

Skehan, P. W., Structures in Poems on Wisdom: Proverbs 8 and Sirach 24. CBQ 41 (1979), 365–379.

Skladny, U., Die ältesten Spruchsammlungen in Israel, 1961.

Smelik, E. L. (in hon.), Ethiek als Waagstuk, 1969.

Smend, R., Die Weisheit des Jesus Sirach: Hebräisch und Deutsch, 1906.

Snijders, L. A., The meaning of zar in the Old Testament: An Exegetical Study, OTS 10, 1954, 1–154.

Stamm, J. J., Dreißig Jahre Dekalogforschung, ThRNF 27 (1961), 189–239.

Stecher, R., Die persönliche Weisheit in den Proverbien, Kap 8, Zeitschrift für Katholische Theologie 30 (1953), 424ff.

Stevenson, W. B., A Mnemonic Use of Numbers in Proverbs and Ben Sira, Transact. Glasgow Univ. Or. Soc 9 (1938/39), 26–38.

Story, C. I. K., The Book of Proverbs and Northwest Semitic Literature, JBL 64 (1945) 319–339.

Taylor, A., The Proverb, 1931.

Thomas, D. W., Notes on some Passages in the Book of Proverbs, JTS 38 (1937), 400–403.
Notes on some Passages in the Book of Proverbs, VT 15 (1965), 271–279.

Thompson, J. M., The Form and Function of Proverbs in Ancient Israel, 1974.

Toombs, L. E., Old Testament Theology and the Wisdom Literature, JBR 23 (1955), 193–196.

Torczyner, H., The Riddle in the Bible, HUCA 1 (1924), 125–149.

Toy, C. H., The Book of Proverbs, 1959⁵.

Uys, P. de V., Justice and Righteousness towards the less Privileged in the Book of Proverbs, NGTT 9 (1968), 183–185.

Van den Born, A., Wijsheid van Jesus Sirach, 1968.

Van der Weiden, W. A., Le Livre des Proverbes, BibOr 23 (1970).

Van der Woude, A. S., De Thora in de Thora, 1967.

Van Oyen, H., Ethik des Alten Testaments, 1967.

Von Rad, G., Die alttestamentliche Satansvorstellung, ThWNT 11, 71–74.
Weisheit in Israel, 1970.
Theologie des Alten Testaments, 1969⁶.
Josephsgeschichte und ältere Chokma, VTS I, 1953, 120–127.

Vriezen, Th. C., An Outline of Old Testament Theology, 1962³.

Wagner, V., Rechtssätze in gebundener Sprache und Rechtssatzreihen im israelitischen Recht, 1972.

Warmuth, G., Das Mahnwort. Seine Bedeutung für die Verkündigung der vorexilischen Propheten Amos, Hosea, Micha, Jesaja und Jeremia, 1976.

Weinfeld, M., The Origin of the Apodictic-Law, VT 23 (1973), 63–75.
Deuteronomy: The Present State of Inquiry, JBL 86 (1967), 249–262.

Weischedel, W., Skeptische Ethik, 1975.

Westermann, C., Der Aufbau des Buches Hiob, 1956.
Weisheit im Sprichwort, in: Schalom – Studien zu Glaube und Geschichte Israels (ed. K-H. Bernhardt), 1971, 73–85. (= Gesammelte Studien, II 1974.)
Das Alte Testament und Jesus Christus, 1968.

Whybray, R. N., The Intellectual Tradition in the Old Testament, 1974.
Wisdom in Proverbs, 1965.
The Book of Proverbs, 1972.

Wiesmann, H., Das Buch der Sprüche, in: Die Heilige Schrift des Alten Testaments, 6/1 1923.

Williams, R. J., The Fable in the Ancient Near East (in FS Irwin), 1956, 3–26.

Wiseman, D. J., Israel's Literary Neighbours in the 13th Century BC, JNSL 5 (1977), 77–91.

Wolff, H. W., Amos' geistige Heimat, 1964.
Die Begründungen der prophetischen Heils- und Unheilssprüche, ZAW 52 (1934), 1–22.
Dodekapropheten I. Hosea, 1965².
Anthropologie des Alten Testaments, 1977³.
Zur Thematik der elohistischen Fragmente im Pentateuch, EvTh 29 (1969), 59–72.

Wundt, Max, Geschichte der Griechischen Ethik, II 1911.

Würthwein, E., Wort und Existenz, 1970.
Die Weisheit Ägyptens und das Alte Testament, 1959, 2–16.
Der Sinn des Gesetzes im Alten Testament, ZThK 55 (1958), 255–270.

Zeller, D., Die weisheitlichen Mahnsprüche bei den Synoptikern, 1977.

Zimmerli, W., Das Gesetz und die Propheten, 1969².
Ort und Grenze der Weisheit in Rahmen alttestamentlichen Theologie, in: Gottes

Offenbarung, 1963 (= Les Sagesses du Proche-Orient Ancien, 1963, 121–137.)
Zur Struktur der alttestamentlichen Weisheit, ZAW 51 (1933), 177–204.
Das Gesetz im Alten Testament, ThLZ 85 (1960), 481–498.
Sinaibund und Abrahambund. Ein Beitrag zum Verständnis der Priesterschrift. ThZ 16 (1960) 268–280.
Grundriß der alttestamentlichen Theologie, 1975².

Text References

(Biblical and Apocrypha)

BEIHEFTE ZUR ZEITSCHRIFT FÜR DIE ALTTESTAMENTLICHE
WISSENSCHAFT

Peter Weimar

Untersuchungen zur Redaktionsgeschichte des Pentateuch

Groß-Oktav. X, 183 Seiten. 1977. Ganzleinen DM 82,–
ISBN 3 11 006731 5 (Band 146)

Rolf Rendtorff

Das überlieferungsgeschichtliche Problem des Pentateuch

Groß-Oktav. VIII. 177 Seiten. 1977. Ganzleinen DM 78,–
ISBN 3 11 006760 9 (Band 147)

Charles F. Whitley

Koholeth

His Language and Thought
Edited by Georg Fohrer

Large-octavo. VIII, 199 pages. 1979. Cloth DM 86,–
ISBN 3 11 007602 0 (Volume 148)

Ingrid Riesener

Der Stamm ʾabad im Alten Testament

Eine Wortuntersuchung unter Berücksichtigung
neuerer sprachwissenschaftlicher Methoden

Groß-Oktav. VIII, 294 Seiten. 1978. Ganzleinen DM 132,–
ISBN 3 11 007260 2 (Band 149)

Prophecy

Essays presented to Georg Fohrer on his sixty-fith birthday
6. September 1980. Edited by J. A. Emerton

Large-octavo. VIII, 202 pages, Frontispiece. 1980. Cloth DM 92,–
ISBN 3 11 007761 2 (Volume 150)

Preisänderungen vorbehalten

Walter de Gruyter Berlin · New York

BEIHEFTE ZUR ZEITSCHRIFT FÜR DIE ALTTESTAMENTLICHE
WISSENSCHAFT

Gerald Sheppard

Wisdom as a Hermeneutical Construct

A Study in the Sapientializing of the Old Testament

Large-octavo. XII, 178 pages. 1980. Cloth DM 78,−
ISBN 3 11 007504 0 (Volume 151)

J. A. Loader

Polar Structures in the Book of Qohelet

Edited by Georg Fohrer

Large-octavo. XII, 138 pages. 1979. Cloth DM 62,−
ISBN 3 11 007636 5 (Volume 152)

Walter Beyerlin

Werden und Wesen des 107. Psalms

Groß-Oktav. XII, 120 Seiten. 1978. Ganzleinen DM 62,−
ISBN 3 11 007755 8 (Band 153)

Hans Ch. Schmitt

Die nichtpriesterliche Josephsgeschichte

Ein Beitrag zur neuesten Pentateuchkritik

Groß-Oktav. XII, 225 Seiten. 1979. Ganzleinen DM 86,−
ISBN 3 11 007834 1 (Band 154)

Georg Fohrer

Studien zu alttestamentlichen Texten und Themen

Groß-Oktav. X, 212 Seiten. 1981. Ganzleinen DM 84,−
ISBN 3 11 008499 6 (Band 155)

Preisänderungen vorbehalten

Walter de Gruyter · **Berlin · New York**